To my

Thanks for your order!

Blessings

Donald Jackson

Religious Lies - Religious Truths

ISBN-10: 1-4752-4398-7
EAN-13: 9781475243987

# Religious Lies - Religious Truths
## It's Time To Tell The Truth!

### Donald Luther Jackson

2012

# Dedication

**Dedicated to Dorothy Ann Jackson**

**Who loves Unconditionally!**

# Endorsements

Don Jackson's writing reflects a personal, passionate and compelling journey to recover the inner meaning of Christianity which has been twisted, abused and distorted beyond recognition in the name of orthodox Christianity. Jackson joins an enlarging chorus of believers who know that if we are to reclaim any authenticity to the message and voice of Jesus, we will have to shed ourselves of the prejudices and bigotry which are being perpetuated in the name of Christianity. To those for whom the practice of faith has led them into the shadows of spiritual alienation, this book will bring light and hope. R. Kirby Godsey, Ph.D., Past President, CEO and Present Chancellor of Mercer University, author of two books, *Is God a Christian?* and *When We Talk about God, Let's Be Honest.*

It is remarkable that people living in the 21ⁿᵈ century still need to be reminded that Jesus is at once an historic figure who lived and died in the half-light of antiquity, a mythological figure created by the Church to answer questions nobody is asking any more, and an heroic interpretation of the best elements in human nature which can be emulated in daily life. Donald Jackson's provocative new book, *Religious Lies—Religious Truths,* is both destructive and constructive. It drives a stake into the heart of fundamentalism while holding out for a renewed Christianity based on the best elements in the teachings attributed to Jesus. Jackson identifies Jesus as "...an archetype...a combination of fact and myth." And he rightly observes, "Were the historical Jesus to return to this earth today, he would not recognize himself." *Religious Lies—Religious Truths* powerfully brings into focus a Jesus whom we can recognize today.

I found myself agreeing with some of Jackson's points, disagreeing with others, but completely delighted that he has brought this lively theological discussion to the dinner table of the Christian family. Thomas W. Shepherd, D. Min., Faculty Member, Historical and Theological Studies Unity Institute and Seminary, Author of *Jesus 2.1: An Upgrade for the 21st Century* and *Friends in High Places.*

# Endorsements

Don Jackson, in his new, earth shaking book has made a quantum leap in moving from the bondage of the mistaken identity of sin/salvation theology to the clarification of the teachings of Jesus as being the restoration of actual Human Life, our true identity as at least as the potential, if not the actual living Christ presence. I highly recommend this book to every person who is on a serious spiritual quest. dr. michael ryce, author of *Why Is This Happening to Me... AGAIN?!*

In "Religious Lies-Religious Truths," Don Jackson repositions the historical arguments about classical Christianism and the original teachings of Jesus. Anyone, especially those considering the Christian ministry, ought to read this important work. The spiritual formation Jackson proclaims lies not in tradition and culture, but opening oneself to the progressive message for which Jesus lived and died. The book is a poignant reminder that this is a crucial moment in which we live regarding knowledge, consciousness, and dedication to truth. Rev. Dr. Vincent W. Carroll, Capt., USN, (ret.) is the author of three books of poetry and is Pastor of Little Stone Church on Mackinac Island, MI.

This book was written for "original" Christians, who were first called that in Antioch (Acts 11:26) because they loved so much. D.A. Jackson, Minister and Poet.

# ACKNOWLEDGMENTS

Several friends assisted me in editing my manuscript. Chief Editor was Lynne Stansell of Sarasota, Florida. Her assistance was extremely beneficial in matters of grammar and construction. Others who previewed my text and offered advice on content and style are Galen Chadwick and Magdelena Preston. To my many friends in Sarasota, Florida, who encouraged me to write this book, especially Josephine Bryant.

# Table of Contents

# Preface

### Religious Lies—Religious Truths
### It's Time To Tell The Truth!

Living this book was a very painful journey for me. Having been born and raised in the fundamental fear-based doctrines of "Christianism," it initially shook the ground on which I stood and left me uncertain and insecure for many decades. Then, it dawned on me that the secure and certain ground on which I once stood was an illusion, a lie perpetrated by those in control Who incarcerated my mind in a propaganda prison made of walls of fear and half-truths, ignorance, and errant, supposedly unquestionable traditions. The research for my book challenged my belief system, undermined my faith and confidence in my once great country, and set me on an adventure that left my brain spinning.

It was my "search for truth" that guided my steps in writing this book. Since truth is a personal and Individual pursuit, readers may find comfort in learning that a growing number of the world's populations are seeking the evidence that this book presents. It is this audience of open-minded, truth-seeking people to whom I address this book. Mine is a polemic to awaken, not merely to inform. Christianity was originally about awakening, not protecting a belief system.

Thomas Jefferson is my hero. Although Jefferson's vision for the American Republic may be dead, his is still the ideal toward which we aspire for spiritual as well as political grounding. The survival of our planet is at stake. The ship of traditional Christianity is floundering and many are lowering the lifeboats looking for an alternate vessel. Orthodox Christianity has failed![1] It has struck the iceberg of pragmatism and in so doing has lost its relevancy. It simply does not work and does not speak to the people of the 21st century. While the church is sinking, its crew is feverously rearranging the deck chairs on the Titanic. Conflict in local churches from Baptist to Unity congregations is testimony to the fact that the Cartesian subject-object model of religion is not viable. It has become caught up in and controlled by egocentric blindness to Truth. The original Christianity of Jesus began in Palestine as a spiritual movement. It moved to the Western world and became a business. It is time to confront this business venture, identifying itself as a church. Let us gather the courage to abandon the economic motivation for the church's survival and embrace Jesus' original blueprint for spiritual evolution.

The alternative to this failed model is trans-personal Christianity or what Ken Wilber calls "Integral Christianity." This is a shift that would resurrect Christianity by creating a "new creature." This intentional, conscious, self-aware, and responsible human being is a participant in transformation that expresses itself in community. This involvement would create an inter-subjective community which abandons the emphasis on individualist spirituality that has focused on ego-involvement. Martin Buber asserts that there are two fundamental ways for us to be in the world, as subjects relating to objects (in order to use them for ourselves) or as subjects relating to subjects (which recognize ourselves in that which meets us at the other end of the "relation").[2]

The purpose of a transpersonal Christianity is to restore an independent transpersonal culture. To be authentic, one must find ways to escape the belief-based approach to religion. Radical self-responsibility is the hallmark of the adult and the adult culture. Authentic spiritual life begins with a trans-event. The trans-perspective does not repudiate, eliminate, or demand the abandonment of experiential consciousness as a private, inner aspect of spirituality. It merely subordinates those stages to the spiritual stages that follow. Wilber points out in his book, *Integral Philosophy* [3], that our progression involves a dialectic process of transcending each preceding stage of growth. Our development is like unpacking a nested set of Russian dolls; one stage lives within another. Many members of the church are at the child stage of development[4] and seem to be unwilling to grow to the next stage. It is this group that is preventing many clergy from embracing "Integral Christianity." This failure is a matter of economics.

---

# Introduction

In 325 C.E. a group of 220 men met and voted. That vote changed Christian history. At the Council of Nicaea, the group promoted Jesus to God, thus creating a new religion that has defined orthodox Christianity since that moment. The religion that was created in this council deviated from the original teachings of Jesus, since those teachings were "too difficult" for the masses to emulate. This substitute Christianity, which I call "Christianism," has failed to change the world. It is a religion of accommodation. It will accommodate itself to any political system that will call itself Christian, as witnessed by the Holy Roman Empire. This new religion of Christianism has been accepted by the masses as the true religion of Jesus; and without any question, these adherents have accepted the dogmas that define this new interpolator.

In the intervening centuries the world has experienced the dark ages, inquisitions, crusades and religious intimidation orchestrated by the leaders of this new religious impostor. All of this was done in the name of the one who came to teach a new philosophy of love, forgiveness and reconciliation. Is America really a Christian nation? Thirteen major wars and the attempted American Indian genocide stand as a contradiction to such a claim.

In this book, I present documented evidence that the claim of "Christianism" is neither unique nor original, but an elaborate fabrication. I was a product of this fabrication, serving as an ordained Southern Baptist Minister for the first fourteen years of my professional career. In the fall of 1967, I resigned my pastorate of a suburban church in Richmond, Virginia. This resignation was prompted by a conflict in the church over my suggestion that we invite the local African

American church to participate in a fifth Sunday evening group service. The venom expressed by my closest friends was a complete surprise to me. Our church had ongoing foreign missions in Africa, and I assumed that there was correlation between those efforts and allowing a black to sit in our church. To my knowledge, there is not a single African American attendee in that church, to date.

After leaving the church, I entered the field of higher education, obtaining a professorship at Ramey College, an extension of Inter American University in Puerto Rico. I was so embarrassed over the obvious contradiction of what the church taught and what the church practiced, that I referred to myself during that period as a "Christian agnostic", taking my cue from Leslie Weatherhead's book by that title. After several years of traveling to Chapel Hill, North Carolina, for summer Ph.D. courses in my field of Counseling Psychology, the government closed Ramey Air Force Base and I lost my position.

I next pursued several business ventures, including Divisional Sales Management positions in two different national corporations. This was my period of discontent. I soon discovered that my spiritual flame had not been extinguished, even though I was still disillusioned with conventional Christianity. I moved to Florida in 1985, discovered the Unity Movement and became an ordained Unity Minister in 1989. My wife, Dorothy Ann, and I served as co-ministers of the Unity Church of Sarasota for twenty-one years, until my retirement in 2007.

This book has been in process most of my adult life with the written completion accomplished within a period of two months. Although it may be controversial, I was driven to write this book with the same intensity that Martin Luther wrote when he said, "Here I stand! I can do nothing else." In this light, my writings may well be a manifesto, calling for a radical change in perspective or a new paradigm.

I will draw a contrast between Christianity and "Christianism," showing the dramatic difference between a religion that follows Jesus, and one that follows the Apostle Paul and the Nicaea Creed. This contrast is revealed in a message on a church marquee: "Life is not a playground; it is a battleground." The followers of "Christianism" practice the philosophy of the lyrics from the song, "Onward Christian Soldiers". The lyrics include the line, "marching on to war, with the cross of Jesus going on before." The symbols found in this song represent the history of Christianism, revealing an agenda that has repudiated the simple yet difficult teachings of Jesus about peace, love, and reconciliation. There are some within this tradition who do not share the traditional misrepresentation of Jesus' message; however, their voices are often silenced or marginalized by a powerful hierarchy or repudiated by the faithful followers within the church.

The material in this book will challenge traditional Christians to examine the evidence that so many scholars have presented and most Christian Ministers learned in seminary. It is surprising and bewildering to realize how this evidence has been completely ignored by the American clergy, who graduated from mainstream seminaries. I trust that many ministers will read this book and grapple again with evidential issues to which they were introduced while in seminary. Extraordinary claims require extraordinary evidence, which the proponents of "Christianism" have failed to deliver. The claim of "Christianism" for uniqueness and originality tends to rely on internal evidence that exists only in a vacuum and totally ignores the evidence of history and external sources.

One writer is scathing in his assessment of blame for the decline of our culture. The author claims that past cultures have risen and fallen throughout history and when they fall, it has always been by their own hands. According to Joseph Chilton Pearce (*The Biology of Transcendence*),[5] the biggest roadblocks to this evolution are religion and science, which together promote violence and arrogance. These "two mongrels" of culture have long forced civilized people into a false either/or choice, one that Pearce characterizes as a choice "between being hanged or shot." For Pearce, the two disciplines have produced "a single mono-culture sweeping the globe and bringing a mounting tide of irrational and ever more intense violence," and leaving us—and especially our children—"spiritually starved."[6]

In the following pages, I will show that these extraordinary claims of "Christianism" cannot be substantiated by close examination of the external evidence. I will present evidence that the teachings of Jesus correlate with the teachings of past spiritual masters (such as Buddha, Plato, Moses, Aristotle) and constitute a superior basis for a religion that has universal appeal and sound historical precedence. Although I respect and study the other spiritual masters, Jesus is my spiritual guide and I dedicate my life to following him.

# Chapter 1
# A METAPHOR ABOUT THE RED PILL

The Matrix, the movie: "Take the Red Pill"
Hosea 4:6 " My people are destroyed from lack of knowledge."
John 8:32 "You shall know the truth and the truth shall set you free.
Romans 12:2 "Do not conform any longer to the pattern of this world,
but be transformed by the renewing of your mind."
Jefferson: "Educate and inform the whole mass of the people…
They are the only sure reliance for the preservation of our liberty."

The Matrix is a 1999 science fiction-action film written and directed by Larry and Andy Wachowski. The film depicts a future in which reality as perceived by most humans is actually a simulated reality created by sentient machines to pacify and subdue the human population, while their body heat and electrical activity are used as an energy source. Upon learning this, computer (hacker) programmer "Neo" is drawn into a rebellion against the machines, involving other people who have been freed from the "dream world" and liberated into reality.

In this movie, humanity is enslaved in a pod-like existence. To keep humanity enslaved, the artificial intelligence created a massive interactive virtual reality for them. By controlling the neurons in the people's brains, the Artificial Intelligence managed to deceive them into thinking that this virtual world was the real world, though in reality they were enslaved in cocoon-like pods. Everything seemed real and normal. The neurologically controlled virtual reality that kept them in prison was the matrix. Using the metaphor of the Matrix movie, I will present undeniable evidence that the Christian Church has fed off its people and has enslaved them in a virtual spiritual prison since the fourth century.

The film uses the metaphor of the red and blue pills. The red pill opens one's mind to the reality of the enslaving condition found in the matrix much like the Prodigal Son when he "came to himself."[7] Unlike the pharmaceutical blue pill that stimulates and expands, the Matrix blue pill deadens and anesthetizes. The blue pill keeps one locked in the dream world, which is a virtual reality, created to enslave the masses. The thesis of *The Matrix* goes to the basic assumptions that we have always held. Morpheus, one of the main characters, counsels Neo that he must let go of all fear, doubt and disbelief. The red pill will free his mind, but the blue pill will keep him in a world where he will believe whatever he is told to believe. Blue-pill people are manipulated like puppets controlled by a puppeteer. They have been brain-washed. Blue-pill people allow others to determine what they believe. Blue-pill people allow the state-controlled media to furnish all their political and economic information. The matrix of our world is the system that is controlled by the elite, who make all the decisions for us.

We escape the matrix by taking the red-pill. Morpheus says to Neo, "You have to understand that many people are not ready to be unplugged." In the movie, people were plugged into electric circuits. Many of them are so unsure and hopelessly dependent on the system that they will fight to protect the very thing that is keeping them in bondage. They will fight to protect the very thing that is destroying them.

Morpheus tells Neo that he knows that there is something wrong with his world. "You don't know what it is, but it's there, like a splinter in your mind, driving you mad." We have to become tired of having the matrix controlling us. Neo had to believe that the matrix existed. He had to learn the rules that govern the matrix and how to bend them to his advantage. He had to learn to identify the lies that brought him into bondage and to replace them with the truth. It is conceivable that something we identify as real is actually rooted in falsehood. We are like the humans in the matrix, ignorantly held in captivity by an illusion. We automatically assume that our neurologically constituted experiences reflect truth when it may very well not be true.

About forty years ago, I took the "red pill." There have been times when I wish that I had taken the "blue pill." The "red pill" has introduced me to risk, danger, pain, confusion, doubt and questions. This book addresses the questions that have driven my search for an understanding of religion and other systems that appeal to the rational mind, not just to the emotions. Most religious people operate on their emotions. In fact, intelligence and ignorance are sometimes mutually exclusive. Ignorance occurs when a person refuses to embrace the facts that constitute a challenge to the security and certainty base on which their religion stands. We believe what we believe because it makes us feel good, safe and comfortable. Anything that challenges those beliefs is often met with hostility, resistance, and repudiation. Large segments of the religious establishment have an unwritten law upon their entrance: "Leave your mind at the door."

The Bible gives us a picture of the existence of two different worlds in which we live. There is the world of illusion and the world of reality. Most of us are stuck between these two worlds. To be stuck is limiting, inhibiting and painful to our progressive nature. We have tried to get unstuck, but quite often we remain trapped. Change is not the answer. The more things change, the more they stay the same. The Jesus message is a liberating message. The theme of his message is freedom, joy, and peace. We bounce back and forth between these two worlds.

The metaphor used in the film illustrates the neurological truth that our entire concept of reality is rooted in the electrical/chemical firings of our brain. It is possible that something other than reality is stimulating your neurons to fire the way they do. It is possible that what we interpret as real may not be true. We are held in the clutches of this dream world, and to a large extent, we are held prisoner to the pattern of this world (or the matrix), instead of being true to the person who we really are. We are called to make a decision at this point to examine our lives. As Socrates taught, "The unexamined life is not worth living."[8]

How many of us have been on the quest to examine our life and the nature of reality? "The matrix is the world that has been pulled over our eyes to blind us from the truth." The red pill opened Neo's mind to the bondage of the matrix world in which he lived. Taking the red pill awakens you to the neurologically controlled matrix in which you are a prisoner. Neo knew that Morpheus was right; there was something wrong with his world. It had become a prison for his mind. The Apostle Paul taught that we should not allow the matrix to control our minds, thoughts and concept of reality. "Be changed by the renewing of your mind."[9] The key to liberation is the movement of our minds from the controlled lies of the matrix to the freedom of expanded human consciousness. When Neo took the "red pill," he began to realize just how deep the rabbit hole really was. He became something more than the extension of someone else's programming, just as I became something other than my parent's programming. The matrix is more than deceptive information. It is the way in which this information is sustained through the diversion of our minds away from the truth of what is really happening. The matrix imprisons us not so much by the information we consciously believe, but by the information given and received on an unconscious level. This is often in contrast to what we say we consciously believe.

Simon Peter said, "People are slaves to whatever masters them."[10] We have symbolic matrix chips within us that are obediently carrying out someone else's programming.

Since the matrix is about chips implanted in humanity by the ruling elite, this book is dedicated to the removal of those chips.

# Chapter 2
# The Original Title of this Book was a Lie

Thomas Jefferson: "Fix reason firmly in her seat, and call to her tribunal every fact, every opinion. Question with boldness even the existence of a God; because, if there be one, he must more approve of the homage of reason, than that of blindfolded fear."

The original title of this book was "They Lied to me about Everything." I changed that title to a more positive one, since that title was a lie. Everyone has an opportunity to stumble onto the truth somewhere along the way. One may be asking, "Who is the 'they' in that original title?" It is basically those who are in power, who wish to impose their personal or philosophical will on others by intentionally misleading or lying to the public. In this book, I will address several areas where this lying is the modus operandi of the elite. Elites feed off ignorance, gullibility, superstition, bigotry, hypocrisy, tyranny and so much more when they are perpetrated in the name and under the disguise of "holy religion." One of the underlying themes of this book is the axiom, "perception determines reality." You cannot see unless your eyes are open. Yeshua (Jesus) often spoke about those who, "having eyes, did not see and ears, did not hear." Most people identify with the lyrics of Simon and Garfunkel's song, *The Boxer*: "Though my story's seldom told. I have squandered my resistance for a pocket full of mumbles. Such are promises, all lies and jests. Still, a man hears what he wants to hear and disregards the rest." It is my prayer that this book will give you the gift of new eyes and ears and that you will not disregard the evidence presented in these pages.

The Religious Lie is one of the most damaging of all lies. The phrase "religious elite" is an oxymoron. It implies that there are those who know how I need to be connected to my source better than I. This connection is the essence of all religions. When I was a little boy, my family perpetuated the Santa Claus myth, creating an unbelievable charade with Santa Claus as the chief character. I was so caught up in "believing" in Santa Claus that the thought of deception never crossed my mind. Christmas morning was a very special time at our house. We jumped from our beds every Christmas into a room filled with presents. Nothing was wrapped. Everything was there just as Santa left it. Part of the elaborate charade was the glass of buttermilk and cake that we left for Santa Claus. The absence of the cake and the empty glass was the "proof" that I needed to bolster my belief in the Santa visitation. I believed in Santa Claus with all my heart and was crushed when I had infallible proof that what I had been told about Santa was not true. I shall never forget the year that I learned the truth about Santa. Until that Christmas Eve when I saw my dad putting together the bicycle that Santa Class delivered to me the next morning, I was a true believer. Then, my world of childhood faith collapsed. I was devastated!

I shall always remember when I discovered the truth about Santa Claus. I thought to myself, "They lied to me about Santa Claus." Although I know, today, that the word, "lie" is too harsh a term for what they did, that's how I felt as a young lad. It took the evidence of sight that led me to my enlightenment about Santa. My parents were merely parroting what they were taught by the religious elite, whose titles range from the Pope to pastor. Since then, I have come to realize that no real harm was done to my psyche by the perpetuation of the Santa Claus legend and I was not abused by a belief system that held so firmly to a literal interpretation of Jesus' life and ministry. All of this was a very important and valid part of my growing from childhood to adolescence. Tragedy would have occurred if I had continued to believe in the truthfulness of Santa Claus as an annual visitor who showered me with gifts. Santa Claus was a "true lie." He is a lie, since there is no single person who flies with his reindeer and descends chimneys (even when none exists). However, he is true, since every person who gives a gift out of love is expressing the spirit of Santa Claus. There are as many Santas as there are people who express the true spirit of Christmas. Yes, Virginia, there is a Santa.

The same scenario occurred in my spiritual odyssey. I was taught that the Bible was the inerrant, infallible word of God. I grew up with a "born again" religious indoctrination, believing in the "washed in the blood, Jesus saves" comfort and security of "old time religion." When I went to seminary, my main motivation was to receive a religious education so that I could defend the faith of my fathers. Then I was exposed to Biblical scholarship, textual criticism, and tools that challenged my naive religious faith. I was confronted with evidence, similar to the bike in the garage experience of my youth. It was evidence that was beyond my ability to rationalize the "old time religious beliefs" of my past. I compared the two experiences and said to myself, "If they lied to me about Santa Claus, they probably lied to me about Jesus."

Since then I have come to believe that nobody lied to me about anything. They simply were following what they had been taught and had no information that would challenge their naïve faith. I will never forget the mournful lament of my mother when she said, "Don, seminary has ruined you." Yes, my parents and the church of which they were a part were sincere. Using the Latin derivation of the word, sincere, they were certainly not without wax. You may not know the practice of ancient furniture makers, who fashioned a piece of furniture out of a faulty piece of wood. They would cover the holes with wax and then seek to veneer the covered piece. If someone wished to discover the authenticity of the piece, they would place it in the sun. The sun would melt the wax and reveal the charade. The charade of Christianity began in the latter part of the third century and the beginning of the fourth. What happened to Christianity in those two centuries is not only an essential part of the whole story of Christian history; it is, in fact, the indispensable key to any correct understanding of the entire history of Christianity. It is perhaps no overstatement to assert that no history has ever been written less objectively than that of the Christian movement.

Winners write history; and because they were winners, the Orthodox Church wrote the history of the Christian movement from their perspective. They were able to crush the dissenting voices of the church that they labeled heretics. Who knows what direction the message of Jesus would have taken had the voices of early Christianity coexisted under mutual respect for individual differences. Perhaps the Jesus story would have disappeared from human history had the uncompromising organization that carried the Jesus story relented. After all, the Christ story has existed for centuries under different religious names, but the insistence that Christianity was unique and original was the major reason for its survival quality and dominance (see chapter 6). Ideas are not the mainspring of human action; emotions are. If one can package an idea in an emotional container, then the chance of universal acceptance is assured. Religious people of every persuasion concern themselves with ideas only as an expression of their belief system. They develop a belief system and then try to defend it by using ideas as a weapon. Ideas are not the driver of a belief system, emotional attachment or aversion is. If one can create a religion where the emotional attachment is tied to a pseudo-intellectual explanation of that belief system, then the chances for its survival increase exponentially. This is witnessed by the serious discussion of early theologians about how many angels can dance on the end of a pin. Most religious zealots want an easy and simple answer; they are unwilling to "go down the rabbit hole." It is just too threatening.

Religion began when the early human started to ask existential questions about his/her existence that was motivated by the fear of death. Such questions generated answers that seemed to satisfy the questioner for a period of time until the events of daily living necessitated new questions. Voices in the early church grappled with these Jobian[11] questions and began to ask about humanity's place and destiny in the universe. They came to opposite conclusions; one was a simple belief based on a closed-ended, dogmatic explanation of destiny, while the other was more complicated and challenging since it was open-ended and shrouded in mystery. One group accepted what others say about truth especially if it is written in a sacred book; while the other group only accepted truth when it could be judged in the arena of human experience. One opinion tells you which way to go and what to think; while the other opinion refrains from telling you which way to go, how to think, and what to do. One group packages truth; while the other knows that ultimately truth can never be contained, since it is realized only in the experience of the search. This book is about ending that search.

There has never been a time in my life when Jesus was not important to me. For forty years, I sought ways to save the baby and throw out the bath water. There were times when I threw out both the baby and the water. I have learned that there is a major difference between Jesus and the commentary of the early church about him. I am seeking diligently to make a distinction between the Jesus of history and the words about him that obscure his reality. I know that there is a major difference between the Jesus of history and the Christ of faith. The first is a flesh and blood person who sought to know God and revealed that understanding in a unique way. The second is a belief system that has obscured the original message and meaning of the man who was a unique Son of God.

The phrase "Son of God" is not original to Christianity. It is part of the language of many religions of antiquity. Alexander the Great was called "the son of God." The Hebrews used the phrase, sometimes as a designation for the nation of Israel. The reference in John 3:16 is a mistranslation of the Greek phrase. It is rendered "only begotten" in the KJV, while the Greek text renders it a "unique Son of God." If Jesus were co-eternal with God, as John's first chapter implies, then that would negate being an "only begotten Son of God." The two texts are incompatible. This is the first of many contradictions that would force me to re-evaluate my literalistic upbringing. The first basic adjustment for me was the emotionally shattering conclusion that the Bible was a human book, filled with mistakes and contradictions, containing myths, legends and stories that were fabricated. I realized that I was surrounded by a cocoon of comfort that my early religious faith provided for me. It was out of this cocoon that I emerged through metamorphosis that liberated me into the insecurity and uncertainty of freedom. History will prove, in my opinion that these religious systems are not so much wrong as they are irrelevant to a mature faith that does not need to believe in any hero out there.

In general, the majority of people in the Western world has been and still is kept in deep ignorance of the truth of the history of their own faith. The religion that started under the name of Christianity in the first century did not long retain its original character and substance. No argument can dispute the assertion that it was not by any means the same religion in the fourth century that it had been in the first. It began with the fourth gospel writer, John, masquerading as a chronicler of the life of Jesus, but ostensibly writing a theological treatise that cannot be taken as literal fact.

One has only to compare the fourth gospel of John with the synoptic gospels to see the glaring difference. The writer of the book of John confesses his bias in the last chapter where he admits that he is writing to convince people that Jesus is the Son of God, not a very objective intention for an historian. But then, what real scholar believes that John was writing history? This leads to an examination of the book that is considered by many to be the authoritative Word of God, the Bible.

# Chapter 3
# A BOOK BY GOD OR A BOOK ABOUT GOD

"The whole history of these books
(i.e. the Gospels) is so defective
and doubtful that it seems vain to
attempt minute inquiry into it:
and such tricks have been played
with their text, and with the
texts of other books relating to them,
that we have a right, from
that cause, to entertain much doubt
what parts of them are genuine.
In the New Testament there is internal
evidence that parts of it
have proceeded from an extraordinary
man; and that other parts
are of the fabric of very inferior minds.
It is as easy to separate
those parts, as to pick out diamonds
from dunghills."
Source: Letter of Thomas Jefferson to John Adams, January 24, 1814

Toto, I don't think we're in Kansas anymore. Dorothy, Wizard of Oz

The Bible has always been the center of my life and my career. I have read it several times from cover to cover and have poured over the teachings of Jesus for endless hours. It played a profound role in my childhood, from the daily Bible readings of my mother to the Bible stories told in my Sunday school class. I never questioned the validity of these stories and never challenged their integrity. The Bible had a prominent place in our home, adorning the central table in the living room on which no other book or object could be placed. I received my own Bible with my name imprinted on the cover upon my high school graduation. Of course this was a red-letter edition, identifying the words of Jesus, which gave them ultimate authority. I used this Bible when I was a teenage "flaming evangelist" notching "saved souls" in the empty pages of my Bible much as the cowboy notched victims on the stock of his rifle. I went to seminary with the sole motivation of receiving an education so that I could defend the faith of my father/mother against the attacks of vicious liberalism. I viewed anyone who even questioned the words of the Bible as an enemy of my faith, who deserved my sternest rebuke if not worse.

I shall never forget when I first became aware that I was wrong about something. Remember, I grew up in a tradition where you had to be right about everything. To be wrong about just one thing would bring into question one's entire belief system, and this was just not permissible.

This revelation occurred in my Greek class during my first year of seminary. We were examining the text where King Agrippa[12] was addressing Paul about his missionary message. In the church of my youth we sang the invitation hymn, "Almost Persuaded," as an emotional appeal for souls to be saved, using this text as our Biblical justification. My minister had a strange habit of extending the invitation to "just one more verse of Almost Persuaded." He would often say, "Now this is the last one" as if your soul rested in the balance. He would then go on to sing several more verses, contradicting his promise, which raised questions in my young mind about his integrity. In my Greek class we learned that the correct translation reflected a tone of sarcasm in Agrippa's response: "Do you think that you are going to make a Christian out of me in a short time?" I was devastated and totally disillusioned, but this class was the beginning of my spiritual journey that led me to an open examination of everything, including the Bible.

The Bible is an ordinary book with an extraordinary message. A proper analogy to explain this conclusion is the analogy of mining for gold. You don't take the dirt that holds the gold ore home with you. You take this ore and you smelt it into purified gold. So it is with the Bible. The nuggets of gold which are the extraordinary message of the Bible are buried deeply in the soil of Hebrew history, which includes special political agendas, a chosen-people mentality, and an angry God who orders the genocide of an entire people. It includes pronouncements that disenfranchise entire groups of people such as women, homosexuals and foreigners. Much that we reject today as being unethical and even illegal is included in the Bible as standard operating procedures, such as polygamy, slavery, and lying.

A good illustration of a religious lie is found in Genesis 34, where the Shechemites were willing to become converted to Judaism through circumcision. This was all a part of a love affair between a Jew and a Shechemite. The Jews promised the Shechemites that they would all become one people allowing inter marriage. All of the sons of Shechem submitted to circumcision at the hands of the Jews. The Bible says quite candidly: "Three days later, while all of them were still sore, the Jews took their swords and attacked the unsuspecting city, killing every male. They looted the city and seized their flocks and herds and donkeys and everything else of theirs in the land. They carried off all their wealth and all their women and children, taking as plunder everything in the houses."[13] They deceived (lied) to this group who were willing to become converts to the Jewish religion, and they did this in the name of their God and their religion. Unfortunately, this has not been an exception in the history of religion, even the religion of the Bible.

I do not see the Bible as divine in origin, nor do I view some parts as divine and some as human. It is all a human product, though born out of a quest to understand the divine/human encounter. Let's look at other parts of the Bible that make it an ordinary book. A great deal of space, especially in Genesis, is consumed with genealogies. An entire book is devoted to a description of the sacrificial system and meticulous laws that must be kept in every detail. There are tall tales that probably were never taken as literal truth by the ordinary Jew of that day. There are the plagues of Egypt,[14] the floating of a steel ax head,[15] a wall that came tumbling down due to a trumpet sound,[16] a man who made the sun stand still,[17] a large body of water that parted allowing the Israelites to walk on "dry" land,[18] a talking donkey,[19] curses that are placed in the mouth of God against the enemies of the Jews,[20] a woman who turned to a pillar of salt simply because she looked back,[21] a rod that turns into a snake,[22] a strange story about testing God with a fleece,[23] the picture of a strong man who killed over a thousand men with the jaw bone of an ass,[24] mercilessness of Jehovah,[25] no mercy by the Jews at God's command,[26] deception by divorce mandated by the high priests because of inter marriage that resulted in families being torn asunder,[27] and Jewish erotic literature that would make a sailor blush.[28]

The sacred books of religion are both a blessing and a curse. They are a blessing when the books are used as maps to plot the spiritual journey of the believers and adherents. With this view, the books tell the story of mankind's attempt to understand and connect with a power beyond his/her comprehension. In this light, religion will always be a mystery, and the sacred books will reflect this humility. They are a curse when adherents take them literally and try to enforce their subjective meaning on others. This includes the Bible as well as the Quran. The Bible is often used as a weapon. "They beat me over the head with the Bible" is a criticism that is raised against religious fanatics who use the Bible in inappropriate ways.

The words in a book are subjective reflections of individual experiences. The Bible, which means book, is a compilation of many different writers from different eras, reflecting different points of view. The Bible has been called the "Word of God." The only way any book can be considered the Word of God is by a faith assertion that ignores rational examination. The belief system that insists that the Bible is the Word of God is quite insistent in its point of view. "If it's in the Bible, you can believe it," is a claim often espoused by fervent believers. "If you can't find it in Scripture, forget it" is a mindset that ignores fatal flaws in the book they claim to be God's word. Even among those who claim that the Bible is the "inspired, inerrant Word of God," there are vast differences in what they believe the Bible actually says. Virtually all of these groups profess to base their beliefs and practices on the Bible, and many consider themselves the true church, to the exclusion of all others.

There is abysmal ignorance among those who profess to believe most in the authority of the Bible. Ask any modern Christian if they believe the Bible is the "Word of God," and they will respond affirmatively. However, ask them to name the books of the New Testament and they will reveal their lack of knowledge. When I was a Southern Baptist minister of a small church in Bealeton, Virginia, I was excited to share with the congregation what I had learned in seminary. It did not take me long to realize that they did not want to hear what I had learned. In one Bible study class, a woman told me, "If the King James Version was good enough for Paul and Silas, then it was good enough for her." These are not stupid people, they are uninformed; and many who are informed, refuse to question their entrenched belief system since it may rock the foundation of their emotional attachment to these preconceived ideas.

Many believers ask the question, "How do we know the Bible is true?" I believe the Bible is true, but I do not believe that it is always factual. As we develop this chapter, the reader will begin to understand the difference between truth and fact. The truth is found in the direction that the writers are moving. They are attempting to explain an experience of a transcendent reality that they cannot explain, and they use inadequate words to make their point. The truth is not to be found in the words, but in the spirit of the writers who seek in their writings to bring humankind closer to its Source.

People believe what they want to believe, mainly because certain belief systems make the individual feel comfortable and secure. Most Christians interpret the Bible in ways that are comfortable to them, but their interpretation may not reflect the original meaning of the text. Many Christians believe that the Bible is the word of God, because the Bible says so. That is circular reasoning and cannot stand up to scholarly examination, especially when it is talking about another book (the Hebrew Bible). The Bible is, indeed, our map; but a map is not the territory. Maps must change as the territory changes, and that is another reason why a book cannot answer all your questions. We are asking questions today that were not addressed in the first century when the Christian scriptures were completed. It is my opinion that the Bible is a question book and not an answer book. Reading the Bible certainly does raise a plethora of questions.

There are several contradictions and incredulities found in the Bible. This was my first clue as a young seminarian at Southeastern Baptist Theological Seminary that the Bible was not the Word of God, but rather a book that contained the Word of God. Let me explain the difference. The Bible, as the Word of God, implies that it is an infallible and inerrant document. Plenary verbal inspiration is a theory that maintains that the Bible is infallible in its original form. What good is it to say that the autographs (i.e., the originals) were inspired? We don't have the originals. We have only error-ridden copies. Since we do not have any original manuscripts, this argument is something of a moot point. I will continue to show some of the many contradictions in the Bible that counter the claim of infallibility and inerrancy which set up the Bible as a false idol.

The story of the virgin birth (told only in Matthew and Luke) gives different accounts of the first eight days of Jesus' life. In Matthew, the writer has the family traveling to Egypt to escape the wrath of Herod the Great, who was threatening the life of the young baby. Luke has the family traveling to Jerusalem on the eighth day for the ceremonial rite of circumcision. These stories are mutually exclusive. In Matthew, the writer maintains that Jesus was born when Herod was Tetrarch of Judea. Luke has Jesus born when Cyrus was governor of Cyreus. Herod died in 4BC and Cyrus was governor in 6 C.E. One author pointed out that the birth of Jesus was not so much a virgin birth miracle as it was a miracle of a ten-year pregnancy. The words of Jesus, allegedly predicting his resurrection, are found in Matthew 12:40 which refer to Jonah residing in the belly of the whale for three days and three nights. According to the resurrection account, Jesus was in the tomb for 36 hours, not the 72 hours of the Jonah event.

Major differences between the Synoptic Gospels and the Gospel of John are so great that one wonders if they were talking about the same events. John's Gospel omits a large amount of material found in the synoptic Gospels, including some surprisingly important episodes: the temptation of Jesus, Jesus' transfiguration, and the institution of the Lord's Supper are not mentioned by John. John mentions no examples of Jesus casting out demons. The Sermon on the Mount and the Lord's Prayer are not found in the Fourth Gospel. There are no narrative parables in John's Gospel (most scholars do not regard John 15:1-8 "the Vine and the Branches" as a parable in the strict sense). John's reference to the raising of Lazarus is totally omitted by the writers of the Synoptic Gospels (a major omission). According to John, Jesus' public ministry extended over a period of at least three and possibly four years. During this time, Jesus travels several times from Galilee to Jerusalem.

The Synoptic Gospels appear to describe only one journey of Jesus to Jerusalem (the final one), with most of Jesus' ministry taking place within one year. John has a high Christology as observed in his first chapter, whereas the Synoptic Gospel writers prefer to refer to Jesus as the "Son of Man." The Synoptic Gospels are descriptive, written in the third person; whereas, John is more reflective and interpretative. Matthew, Mark and Luke are more interested in writing a history of the life of Jesus, whereas John is more evangelical in his approach, stating in his last chapter that he is writing to convince. John uses the method of extensive dialogue, while the Synoptic Gospels utilize short and pithy sayings of Jesus. John employs antithetical dualism using such contradistinctions as light/darkness and life/death symbolism. The Synoptic Gospels' favorite phrase of Jesus is the "kingdom of heaven," whereas the same idea in John employs the phrase, "eternal life." The language style is quite different in John than it is in the Synoptic Gospels. It is difficult to determine where the words of Jesus and the interpretation of the writer of John begins or ends. Most Biblical scholars recognize the Synoptic Gospels as containing history; whereas, they see very little history in the Gospel of John.

It is to be noted that all of the original copies of the four gospels in the Christian Scriptures have been lost. We must rely upon hand-written copies which are an unknown number of hand-copied replications removed from the originals. The oldest known surviving part of a gospel dates from about 125 C.E. It consists of about 50 lines from the Edgerton Gospel, one of the 40 or so gospels that never made it into the official canon, and whose author is unknown. Another portion of an ancient manuscript, containing part of the Gospel of John, is also dated to about 125 C.E., a business-card sized fragment, Codex Sinaiticus[29], is one of the most important books in the world. Handwritten well over 1600 years ago, the manuscript contains the Christian Bible in Greek, including the oldest complete copy of the New Testament. The remaining manuscripts date to the second half of the second century C.E. or later.

Textual scholar Bart Ehrman writes: "It is true, of course, that the New Testament is abundantly attested in the manuscripts produced through the ages, but most of these manuscripts are many centuries removed from the originals, and none of them perfectly accurate. They all contain mistakes—altogether many thousands of mistakes. It is not an easy task to reconstruct the original words of the New Testament."[30]

Many sincere Bible students and scholars are weary of constant revisions of the Scripture, taken from the Greek, and are turning to the Aramaic as a source for their interpretation. It is to be noted that all manuscripts are extinct, including Greek and Aramaic. We only have copies of these documents in both languages. My hypothesis that the original manuscripts of the New Testament were written in Aramaic, not Greek, is an argument from silence. This argument is similar to the argument for the literary construct, known to scholars as Q. The Q source (also Q document or Q) is a hypothetical source for the Gospel of Matthew and the Gospel of Luke. Q (short for the German Quelle, or "source") is defined as the "common" material found in Matthew and Luke but not in the Gospel of Mark. This ancient text supposedly contained quotations from Jesus. The existence of Q has been questioned, but it is highly regarded by scholars as a source of circumstantial evidence. Generally, scholars have not accepted my Aramaic hypothesis, although it is supported from internal examinationOf the texts; e.g. the transliteration of the Aramaic words of Jesus on the cross.

The Peshitta is the Syriac Vulgate, the standard version of the Bible for churches in the Syriac or Eastern Church Tradition. This text sheds light on the influence of Aramaic in Biblical translation. The word Peshitta means clear, sincere, simple and easy to understand. When the King James Version of the Bible was published in 1611 C.E., the ancient Aramaic Bible manuscripts of the Peshitta texts of the Churches of the East written in the Old Estrangela characters were unknown in Europe. Estrangela follows the Hebrews written language in that it contains twenty-two characters while omitting the vowels in the text. Demetrius, the royal librarian, in his report to king Ptolemy of Egypt relative to the Jewish Scriptures states: "The characters in which it is written are like the proper characters of the Syrians (Arameans) and are pronounced like theirs also."[31] These ancient characters of the Estrangela were used by scribes in the Church of the East until the 11th century, when Christians began to use Nestorian letters. The change in the alphabet and the introduction of the vowel system is responsible for many errors which crept into later manuscripts. There are thousands of differences between the ancient Peshitta text and the Western versions of the Bible. Thousands of passages, which were obscure and meaningless through mistranslations, become clear and meaningful when translated from the ancient Peshitta manuscripts.

The Bible is a book containing the Word of God, which implies an existential experience with the One about whom the book was written. The Bible is an attempt to connect the reader with the Power and Presence of the One who is. The Bible is a spiritual map, leading one into a personal experience with God. The Bible is my textbook. I take it seriously, but I do not venerate the book. It is because I take it so seriously that I am willing to expose it to all the textual and scholarly criticism that a book of this caliber deserves. Since it contains the Word of God, it is my responsibility to excavate this treasure, until I am able to separate the soil from the gold. In so doing, I must be able to discern the gold from the dirt. Another metaphor for seeing the bible in a different light comes from the Buddhist tradition. The Bible is like a finger, pointing to the moon. The focus should not be on the finger, but on the moon to which the finger is pointing. Still another metaphor uses the analogy of the window. The window is there to see the scene beyond. One does not focus on the speck of dirt on the window pane, but ignores the speck to enjoy the beauty of the scene that the window reveals. In time, the window has become old, dusty, and opaque. It has become the object, instead of the medium, through which we see. It is made into an altar and has been made the focal point of worship in homes and cathedrals. The Bible points to a relationship with the One to whom the finger points and the window reveals, yet so often we become enamored with the finger or the speck on the window pane. Would it not be better to clean the glass so that we can see through the window and find the ultimate truth that the Bible reveals? Paul hinted at this when he says:

> For we know in part, and we prophesy in part; but when that which is perfect is come, that which is in part shall be done away. When I was a child, I spake as a child, I felt as a child, I thought as a child; now that I am become a man, I have put away childish things. For now we see in a mirror, darkly; but then face to face: now I know in part; but then shall I know fully even as also I was fully known.[32]

Thomas Jefferson made an attempt to focus on the essence of what the New Testament was about when he penned his Jefferson Bible, a distillation of the entire New Testament into a small book that contains the teachings of Jesus and nothing else. For him, this was the Word of God, and it is becoming more so for me. I recently identified myself as a Jesusonian. Maybe I should add, Jeffersonian

Christian, because I believe it is more important to follow Jesus and believe him than it is to believe in him. To believe in him requires little effort, only an intellectual and emotional response to a theological idea about him. To follow him requires a commitment to his way of life, a way of life characterized by love, forgiveness and reconciliation. It is also a way of radical non-violence and anti-materialism. It is a fact of history that the early Christian community was called "followers of the way." It was much later in Antioch that the Jesus followers were called Christians, a term of derision in its original use.

A valid question surrounds the historicity of the Bible. Is it a book of history? According to Alvin Boyd Khun, "There is not one iota of history as we know in the entire Bible."[33] If this is true, then this is good news for it signals the recovery of a much more spiritual belief system and experience of God. A myth is a story that is so true that it transcends the literary vehicle in which it is contained. This is certainly not the common definition by the man on the street, who believes that a myth is something that is false. The Old Testament is not an historically accurate record of events, but rather it is the story of a people's evolving understanding of God and of God's relationship with humanity. The writers of the New Testament used metaphors, myth, poetry, allegory, parables and other devices to describe eternal truths. There is a flaw in the Jesus seminar's approach. They seem to side with the fundamentalist by adopting the mistaken view that we are dealing with history. The Gospels are literary editions of allegorical and mythical themes that have a history of their own but contain little history in them. The gospels, as interpreted by fundamentalists, stand helplessly vulnerable to the attack of plain reason. Tom Harpur adds, "They are indeed exposed as the old manuscripts of the dramatized ritual of the incarnation and resurrection of the sun God, a ritual that was first Egyptian, later Gnostic and Hellenic, then Hebrew, and finally adopted ignorantly by the Christian movement into history."[34]

Part of the Hebrew Bible, or Old Testament as Christians label it, is a redaction or editing of Sumerian and Egyptians texts, which was uncovered by the discovery of the Rosetta Stone. This discovery provided scholars with the ability to read Egyptian hieroglyphs. Without this discovery, we would not have been able to make the connection between Christian, Jewish and other ancient religious texts. The Rosetta Stone is an ancient Egyptian stone of black granite inscribed with a decree issued at Memphis in 196 BC on behalf of King Ptolemy V. The decree appears in three scripts: the upper text is Ancient Egyptian Hieroglyphs, the middle portion Demonic script, and the lowest section Ancient Greek. Because it presents essentially the same text in all three scripts, it provided the key to the modern understanding of Egyptian Hieroglyphs. Prior to the discovery of the Rosetta Stone and its eventual decipherment, there had been no understanding of the Ancient Egyptian language. This is the reason why, prior to 1799 when the stone was discovered, Biblical scholars were limited in making the connection between the New Testament, the Hebrew Bible and ancient texts found on inscriptions carved in the stone walls of ancient sites in Egypt.

Sumerian literature is the literature written in the Sumerian language during the Middle Bronze Age. The Sumerians invented the first writing system, which appeared in cuneiform, a system of symbols. The Sumerian language remained in official and literary use in the Akkadian and Babylonian empires. It is through the science of archeology that we have this evidence, and since it is in stone, it is undeniable evidence. The epic of Gilgamesh is a story about an historical figure that is represented as a demigod of superhuman strength who built the city walls of Uruk to defend his people from external threats and traveled to meet the sage Utnapishtim, who had survived the Great Deluge. He is usually described as two-thirds god and one-third man.

Many scholars claim that the flood narrative of Genesis1:7 is a rewritten version of The Epic of Gilgamesh, from the Enuma Elish produced by the Sumerians. Here is a brief background of the Epic of Gilgamesh. Gilgamesh was an oppressive ruler of the Sumerians, whose people called to the gods to send a nemesis. One nemesis, Enkidu, became friends with Gilgamesh, and the two went out on many adventures. Enkidu was eventually killed, and Gilgamesh then feared for his own life. In his search for immortality, he met Utnapishtim, who had been granted immortality by the gods, following his rescue from the flood. Utnapishtim then recounted the flood and how he became immortal. There are many similarities between the Epic of Gilgamesh and the Genesis story of the flood. There are seven similarities: (1) Flood occurs in the Mesopotamian plain. (2) Main character is warned to build a boat to escape the flood. (3) The main character is told to save himself, his family and a sampling of animals. (4) The boats were sealed with tar. (5) The boats came to rest on a mountain. (6) Birds were released to determine if the water had receded. (7) Main character sacrificed an offering. Although there are some differences in the two accounts, the similarities are so obvious as to be conclusive. Parts of the Hebrew Bible are redactions of these Sumerian accounts, which underscore the authors' claim that the Bible contains little original material and contains very little history. Was the Sumerian account a myth? This is a question that must be asked about the Genesis account, since both tell essentially the same story. It is easier to dismiss the Sumerian story as a myth, but emotional attachment makes it more difficult to apply the same standard to the Biblical story.

I have highlighted only a few references that allude to the fact that the Bible is filled with ordinary material that shows the Jews in a less than favorable light. There are many more, found in numerous books on this subject. This evidence is merely the soil through which we must dig in order to find the "real stuff", the extraordinary message of a book that contains nuggets of gold. If I were given a choice between choosing the Bible or the Constitution of the United States, I would choose the Constitution. The reason for my choice is obvious when one realizes that the freedom to follow the dictates of reason and intuition always supersedes the dictates of an authoritative book, which by logic must be interpreted. The Constitution, especially the Bill of Rights, needs no interpretation, although some Judges seem to think otherwise.

It is difficult to determine whether or not the Bible stories have power because they are true or that they have power because they are so much a part of our culture. The characters in our Bible stories are archetypes for the deeper and different parts of us and that is the reason that they speak to our psyche. Joseph Campbell said, "Christianity is the only religion in history that has insisted on literalizing its stories."[35] Herein lies the problem. If we let the stories remain a literary device designed to carry eternal truths, we would be far wiser. It is only when we insist that these "crazy" stories or metaphors are factual that we stump our religious toes. The Bible is filled with stories that have profound truth, when seen from the standpoint of allowing the original intent. Human beings have a way of embellishing these stories and insisting that we believe them as historical facts.

We have very little problem seeing the magic in a story like the Wizard of Oz, but sometimes we have great difficulty in applying the same standard to the Bible. The Wizard of Oz is one of the best metaphysical movies ever made. Generations have traveled down the Yellow Brick Road to Oz without realizing they were on a spiritual path. The story is part of our culture, just as Bible stories are part of our culture. Who doesn't know about Dorothy and her little dog, Toto? They were carried off by a tornado from black-and-white Kansas and deposited amidst the Munchkins in the merry Ol' Technicolor Land of Oz. You know what follows, right? Glinda, the Good Witch of the North, tells the already homesick Dorothy that she can ask the wonderful Wizard of Oz for help. Along the way, she is befriended by the Scarecrow, who wants to ask the Wizard for brains; the Tin Woodman, who needs a heart, and the Cowardly Lion, who seems to be short on courage. And of course, there's that pesky mean, green Wicked Witch of the West, upset because Dorothy's house landed on her sister and killed her.

Where is the home for which Dorothy seeks, the brain the scarecrow wants, the heart the tin man seeks and the courage the lion requested? They're within, of course! Dorothy and company think that they're off to see the Wizard (who is projected as a kind of God figure) but then they find out that the Wizard isn't what he is reported to be ("I'm a very good man; I'm just a very bad wizard.") The lesson here is that we are not to turn to a God outside us, in a physical heaven or an Emerald City, but rather we are to search within us. As Jesus said, "the kingdom of God is within you."

The Wizard turns out to be a person with some understanding of metaphysics. He helps the Scarecrow, Tin Woodman, and Cowardly Lion realize that what they seek is within, and was always there. He tells the Scarecrow that "anybody can have a brain; that's a very mediocre commodity," and then awards him an honorary Th.D. (Doctor of Thinkology). He inducts the Cowardly Lion into the Legion of Courage for "meritorious conduct, extraordinary valor, and conspicuous bravery against wicked witches." He presents the Tin Man with a heart. Dorothy also learns that the kingdom is within her. Glinda, the Good Witch, who may be seen to represent the presence of the Holy Spirit guiding Dorothy toward that "supreme realization," tells Dorothy that she has always had the power to go home. However, she had to find it out for herself. Dorothy only has to click the heels of the ruby slippers together three times and repeat,

"There's no place like home." The clicks and the repetition are merely focusing tools. Dorothy expresses her knowledge that Truth is within with this famous declaration: "If I ever go looking for my heart's desire again, I wouldn't look any further than my own backyard, because if it isn't there (and it always is), I never really lost it to begin with."

Dorothy, the Scarecrow, the Tin Woodman, and the Cowardly Lion represent the different ways in which we think that we become separated from God. In actuality, of course, we are never separated from God. We all battle forces that seem to come from outside us our Wicked Witches of the East and West and others play into our projections, but we can all learn the value of going within to find our God essence. The character of Dorothy also can stand for our inherent state of goodness and purity as God's whole and perfect children. From this simple innocent state, Dorothy's troubles literally melt away in Oz. Significantly, earlier (on the farm) Dorothy wistfully sings about a place "where troubles melt like lemon drops."

The lessons we learn from the movie are:

- Pay no attention to that man behind the curtain. Imagine Dorothy's surprise when Toto pulled back the curtain and revealed the Wizard was nothing but a regular man, especially after all her trials and tribulations to get to the Emerald City to ask the Great and Powerful Wizard of Oz for help.
- You've always had the power. Glinda expressed it this way: "She had to learn it for herself." When asked by the Tin Man what she learned, Dorothy said, "Well, I...I think that it.... That it wasn't enough just to want to see Uncle Henry and Auntie Em...and it's that if I ever go looking for my heart's desire again, I won't look any further than my own backyard, because if it isn't there, I never really lost it to begin with! Is that right?" This is where the answer lies to all our problems.

- Dorothy comes of age. The four female characters in the movie were all alter egos of Dorothy in her discovery of self and spiritual awakening in order to gain her own strength and identity.

I have used an example of spiritual meaning that is found in a fictional story, the Wizard of Oz. There are several other modern stories that carry mythological meaning, such as "Beauty and the Beast" and "The Phantom of the Opera." Each of these stories is a literary vehicle that carries a special truth. Both deal with the dark side of human personality and how to embrace it. I propose that we use the Bible, especially the teachings of Jesus, in a similar fashion. The teachings of Jesus found in Luke the sixth chapter[36] contain elements of the shadow side of personality. This shadow side of our personality was described by Carl Jung as one of man's recognizable archetypes. According to Jung, the shadow is instinctive and irrational. It is prone to projection, which is our tendency to project our own faults into another person. It is Jesus' log in our own eye; speck in the other person's eye analogy. We do not see reality correctly, because we cannot distinguish between what belongs to us and what belongs to another. Shadow work was what was happening in Jesus' temptation experience. Jesus was dealing with the allure to misuse his power for ego satisfaction. He projected on to the figure, Satan, his inner struggle. He was dealing with his own "log" projected out onto a Satan personification. He was able to own his issues because he was able to embrace his own fallibility. He did say, "Of my own, I can do nothing."[37] The ability to be aware of the existence of the shadow, without identifying with it, is a sure sign of spiritual growth. Confrontation of the shadow is a courageous exercise, but one that reaps rich rewards. Using the teachings of Jesus as the springboard, this new myth will focus on producing a citizen of the kingdom that owns his/her stuff; yet one who is willing to do the work that produces spiritual transformation.

Rudoph Bultmann was one of the first scholars to suggest the de-mythologizing of the New Testament. The goal of de-mythologizing is to eliminate all mythical elements from the Bible so as to arrive at its essential meaning. This includes the attempt to restate the message of the Bible in rational terms, removing the mystical from the text. There are parts of the essential meaning of the Bible that defy rational explanation. It is this area of interest that needs a myth to carry the truths. Instead of de-mythologizing, I suggest that we need a re-mythologizing of the entire Bible, including the New Testament. The task for some scholar, with a creative mind, is to find a new myth in which to carry the truths of the Bible, especially areas with non-rational meaning such as the Transfiguration of Jesus.[38]

To understand the resurrection of Jesus properly, one must understand the true meaning of the transfiguration. Jesus did not become something that he wasn't; he became something that he always was at the transfiguration scene. The miracle of the experience on the Mount was a miracle of perception on the part of the disciples. It was their ability to see Jesus differently that constituted the meaning of the event that foretold the resurrection. What they saw was moving molecules of energy that appeared as light. In Mark 9:9, Jesus told his disciples to say nothing to anyone until after the Son of man has been raised from the dead. This allusion was a revelation of the real meaning of the resurrection. It was and still is a miracle of perception. Their ability to see things differently changed.

It was Origen who saw the connection between the resurrection of Jesus and the transfiguration of Jesus. He knew that a true understanding of the resurrection required a proper understanding of the event that took place on the mount of transfiguration. He knew that a proper understanding of Jesus' resurrection required a proper understanding of the new creature that Paul talked about in his writing. This new creature was not one who believed certain facts about Jesus' death and resurrection. This transformed creature was one who saw things through spiritual eyes. Paul concludes that if the resurrection were not a fact, then his preaching was in vain and our faith was futile.

Unfortunately, Paul interpreted Jesus' resurrection as a resuscitated body, known in theology as the bodily resurrection. In fact, the stories about the events that the Bible recorded after Jesus "rose from the dead," tell a different story. The ending of the book of Mark is revealing, since they show the mindset of the disciples. Mark, the oldest writer of the Synoptic Gospels, ends his gospel with the eighth verse of his sixteenth chapter. After Mark made the proclamation that Jesus rose from the dead, he made the following observation: "And trembling and bewildered, the women went out and fled from the tomb. They said nothing to anyone because they were afraid."[39] The earliest manuscripts and other ancient witnesses do not record verses 9-20.

When Paul confesses that the failure to believe in the bodily resurrection of Jesus negates his preaching, he may have been correct. Perhaps Paul was preaching the wrong gospel. He was preaching a gospel of a faith-based belief system. Jesus preached the gospel of the kingdom of heaven as a present reality, one that saw things differently and as a result treated people differently. If the resurrection of believers is the essential understanding of the meaning of Jesus' resurrection, then it is critical to understand just what this means. He implies that one will not be resurrected unless he believes the proper facts about Jesus' death.

Several Roman Catholic scholars have questioned the validity of the bodily resurrection teaching. One example is the imminent scholar and former professor at Union Theological Seminary, Raymond Edward Brown, who wrote nearly forty books on the New Testament. His book, *A Risen Christ in Eastertime: Essays on the Gospel Narratives of the Resurrection*,[40] addresses the contradictions found in the New Testament regarding the resurrection narratives. The reader is encouraged to examine his account of this topic found in two books from his pen. A surprise finding reveals that Cardinal Ratsinger, presently Pope Benedict XVI, denies the bodily resurrection of Jesus. One Catholic writer accuses him of heresy, maintaining that the Pope does not believe in the Resurrection. This writer[41] claims that the Pope destroys the central miracle of the Christian faith by denying the resurrection. This is, unfortunately, the pitfall of the fundamental mindset. Nowhere in his writings does the Pope say that he does not believe in the resurrection. He maintains a scholarly position claiming that the Gospels do not support flesh and blood resurrection teaching. This teaching is strictly an interpretation of the Apostle Paul.[42]

Let's return to the stories found in the New Testament about Jesus' resurrection. The baffling account found in Luke 24 raises many questions.[43] The Road to Emmaus story contains easily recognizable literary motifs associated with similar stories in Genesis and Judges. In Genesis, Abraham sees three strangers on the road and exercises hospitality by inviting them in to eat with him. It emerges in the course of the narrative that the three strangers were angelic messengers and one is even named "the Lord."[44] Then two of those same strangers travel to Sodom where Lot has to work to persuade them to stay at this place before continuing their journey. It is late in the day, as in the Emmaus road story. He is unaware of their identity until later in the narrative.[45] In Judges 13 we read about an unnamed woman who meets a "man of God", but whom the audience knows is an angelic messenger. Her husband is named, Manoah, and he prays to God to send the same man again but this time "to us"—both of them. So God sent him again but only to his unnamed partner. She had to call Manoah to meet him. The couple, Manoah and his wife, presses the "man of God" who speaks to them of divine promises to come in and stay with them in their house. A sacrifice is offered and the "man of God" reveals his true identity by disappearing before their eyes carried up into heaven by the flames and smoke of the sacrifice. The similarities of this account to the Emmaus Road event are striking.

- Two people receive a visit from a supernatural being.
- Only one of the two persons is named. How readers would love to know the name of both in the two stories. The authors of both are in some way playing with their readers' curiosity.
- The supernatural being speaks of divine plans and knowledge.
- The couple invites this stranger to stay with them and eat.
- A meal or sacrifice is begun.
- Before the stranger eats, he miraculously vanishes before the couple's eyes.
- By witnessing this disappearing trick, the couple is aware of the identity of their guest.
- The couple speaks to each other about their experience and what they have just seen and express their emotional responses.

In the Emmaus Road story, a total stranger walks with several of Jesus' disciples, one is named Cleopas, who appears to be the first to meet the resurrected Jesus. Remember, we have never heard the name Cleopas mentioned in the New Testament before this story. Was Luke hiding the identity of Simon Peter or was this another disciple? It must be remembered that before Luke's gospel was written, there existed no narrative about the resurrected Jesus appearing first and exclusively to Peter. Is it possible that Luke wanted to wrap narrative flesh around the doctrinal "fact" that the very first appearance of the resurrected Jesus was to Peter.[46] Cleopas also has an unnamed companion accompanying him. The mystery is enhanced by naming only the one who was engaged in the actual conversation with

Jesus, at least according to Codex Bezae.[47] The bookend narratives in this same chapter deal with familiar characters in the Jesus story. Luke uses a three-part recognition revelation to announce the resurrection of Jesus, with the Emmaus story being the middle and longer part.

These two disciples walked the Emmaus road and listened to this stranger interpret the Scriptures. At the end of the journey, the stranger vanished and their eyes were opened to the fact that this stranger was indeed the resurrected Jesus. The recognition came after the breaking of the bread, which is a clear reference to the Lord's Supper. Notice the reference to their eyes being opened. This is testimony to the power of perception, the ability to see things differently. The miracle of the resurrection was a miracle of perception. The resurrection of Jesus did not change who Jesus was; it only revealed who he was, a being of light, who could emerge from the tomb without the stone being rolled away and who could also walk through a wall without the door being opened.[48] Flesh and blood does not accomplish such feats, although a belief in the bodily resurrection was common by the end of the first century. This is the reason why the writer, John, told the story about the resurrected Jesus eating bread and fish by the seashore.[49] This story was designed to show, from John's point of view, that the resurrected Jesus had a real body and was not who he revealed himself to be at the Transfiguration.

Our resurrection will not change us; it will only reveal who we are: beings of light and swirling molecules of energy, awaiting our transformation. Jesus said, "Ye are the light of the world."[50] This was not a figurative statement, but a statement of our reality. Paul Smith observes that Jesus was addressing the multitude comprised of pagans, sinners, and ordinary Jews. He lists six amazing things about the crowd that Jesus called the light of the world.[51]

1    Nobody there was a Christian, not even the disciples. Not even Jesus.
2    Most of the crowd was not disciples of Jesus.
3    Many were the outcasts of society.
4    Jesus did not say, "Some of you are the light of the world."
5    Jesus did not say, "You must become the light of the world."
6    Jesus meant that we're the light of the world exactly as he was.

The transfiguration story tells us that Jesus was so in touch with his Christed nature that he could raise and lower his vibration energy at will. This is the meaning of his "light of the world" statements. The transfiguration story in the scripture is about Jesus allowing his disciples, Peter, James and John, to watch him transform into his light body. These three disciples represent love, non-judgment and faith. As we unfold our own Christ nature through these teachings, we, too, begin to unfold the nature that is the Divine within. Our own vibrational energies are lifted into higher frequencies, and we become more of that light. Everyone is the light of the world. The key is the awareness of who you are. Jesus reminded us not to hide this light under a bucketful of ego. God's Spirit wants us to be connected to that light within and to be transformed by it. Your life really matters. Therefore, make it matter. Make it count! The words of the martyred missionary, Jim Elliot, express the truth of the message of Jesus, "Only one life, 'twill soon be past. Only what's done for Christ will last." Remember, the Christ is the indwelling spirit of God; so what you do for Christ, you do for yourself.

# Chapter 4
# SEARCHING FOR THE REAL JESUS

"Among the sayings and discourses imputed to him (i.e. Jesus) by his biographers, I find many passages of fine imagination, correct morality, and of the most lovely benevolence; and others again of so much ignorance, so much absurdity, so much untruth, charlatanism, and imposture, as to pronounce it impossible that such contradictions should have proceeded from the same being." Source: Thomas Jefferson to William Short

What does it mean to be real? This is a question that has been asked by philosophers as well as theologians down through the ages. In the movie, *The Matrix*, there is an exchange between the two main characters, Neo and Morpheus. Neo asked Morpheus, "What is real?" Morpheus responds, "The matrix is control. The matrix is a computer-generated dream world built to keep us in servitude that is designed to change a human being into (and he holds up a battery) something that simply holds a charge." At one point in the film, Neo asks Morpheus if his experience in the matrix is real. Morpheus responds, "How do you define real? If you are talking about what you can feel, smell, taste and see, then reality is simply the electrical signal interpreted by your brain. It is a neurological construct. It is a matrix. Yet, it is just possible that your interpretation of your electrical signals may be wrong." Herein is revealed the premise of *The Matrix* movie.

Unfortunately the authors of the movie do not define the term "real." They only give an example of what is not real, which is the absence of freedom. I suppose that they do define the term in an odd way, since a partial definition of realness is freedom, and then the lack of freedom is the opposite of real. The other aspect of this definition is covered in a dialogue between the rabbit and the skin horse in *The Velveteen Rabbit*:

> "What is REAL?" asked the Rabbit one day, when they were lying side by side near the nursery fender, before Nana came to tidy the room. "Does it mean having things that buzz inside you and a stick-out handle?" "Real isn't how you are made," said the Skin Horse. "It's a thing that happens to you. When a child loves you for a long, long time, not just to play with, but REALLY loves you, then you become real." "Does it hurt?" asked the Rabbit. "Sometimes," said the Skin Horse, for he was always truthful. "When you are real, you don't mind being hurt." "Does it happen all at once, like being wound up?" he asked, "or bit by bit?" "It doesn't happen all at once," said the Skin Horse. "You become. It takes a long time. That's why it doesn't happen often to people who break easily, or have sharp edges, or who have to be carefully kept. Generally, by the time you are real, most of your hair has been loved off, and your eyes drop out and you get loose in the joints and very shabby. But these things don't matter at all, because once you are Real you can't be ugly, except to people who don't understand." "I suppose you are real?" said the Rabbit. And then he wished he had not said it, for he thought the Skin Horse might be sensitive. But the Skin Horse only smiled.[52]

While *The Matrix* film depicts a society living in captivity, *The Velveteen Rabbit* describes a condition characterized by authenticity and love. To be real involves a combination of freedom and authenticity, which embodies the experience of love. Using this as criteria, the real Jesus is the person whose picture is painted by the Synoptic writers in what is known as "the sayings of Jesus." The real Jesus emerges when we allow the purity of his message to overshadow any comments about him. We will never find the real Jesus in any comments about him, including my own. The search must be personal, if it is to be real; otherwise, it is second-hand religion. Or, as expressed in *The Matrix*: "Unfortunately, no one can be told what The Matrix is. You have to see it for yourself."

We may never discover who the real Jesus was to the satisfaction of the entire Christian community since there was intense division and diversity over this subject from the very beginning. Thomas Shepherd comments about this lack of unity in the early church. "When Jesus walked among humanity, he was accompanied by at least twelve disciples, each a one person denomination, endlessly quib-bling over doctrines and personal authority."[53] There was constant bickering and infighting among the various fac-tions of Christianity as the followers of Jesus tried to identify just who he really was. There were questions over his nature including: Was he human? Was he divine? Was he both? If he were both, as a large segment of the Christian commu-nity taught, the question centers on how he could be two separate beings, one human and one divine, at the same time.

These are questions that were eventually resolved by a vote of church leaders in the form of creeds and dogmas, which insisted that Jesus was fully God and fully man. These disputes affected not only the direction of the church, but also the transmissions of the scriptures since the recording scribes were caught up in this ugly theological controver-sy. There is evidence that these scribes altered the texts to fit their theological persuasion, although many changes came through unintended scribal errors as well as deliber-ate modifications.

It is the thesis of this book that we need a Christology that preserves divinity, but one that rejects the claim that this divinity is found only in Jesus of Nazareth. The Methodist minister, Robert Keck, spoke of the need for a "son-set" to occur so that we may have a divine "son-rise" within each of us. Robert Funk of the Jesus Seminar has suggested that Jesus needs a demotion. He believes that the theistic framework in which Jesus has been captured is no longer believable. We need to examine what there was about Jesus' life that caused the theistic interpretation to be thought appropriate in the first place. Bishop Spong believes that the God claim for Jesus must not be dependent on an out-dated God-definition. He believes that a new God defini-tion must resonate with the humanity as well as the divinity of Jesus. Critics claim that this understanding makes Jesus just another human being. It is this phrase, "just another," that I challenge. Jesus was an extraordinary and unique human being.

The theistic interpretation of Jesus is not original in spite of the claim of Christianity that it is unique and exclusive. There are over thirty different religious traditions that have a virgin birth, a death and resurrection story and a salvation motif. The supernatural suit of armor attached to Jesus was not original to the early understanding of who Jesus was. Paul knew nothing of the Jesus as portrayed in the Gospels because they had not been written at the time Paul wrote his letters. In Paul we find little of the theistic framework and little of the imposed supernaturalism that was to develop later. Paul does not embrace an incarnational and Trinitar-ian language of a developed theism that later emerged in the second and third centuries. I recommend that the serious student of Jesus' life and ministry start reading the New Testament in a chronological order and become ac-quainted with the Q material.

Most every Christian knows that Jesus was not a Chris-tian; he was a Jew. He grew up in a Jewish tradition and was part of Judaism, albeit a reformer. He came not to es-tablish a new religion, but to call men to a higher spiritual order, one that he called the kingdom of heaven. The Gospels are essentially Jewish books, written by Jewish people for early (Jewish) Christians who were still worshiping in the synagogue. As a direct result of the destruction of the Temple in 70 C.E., the Christian faith, which had originally been a Jewish movement, began the shift that was destined to redefine Christianity as a bitterly anti-Semitic and anti-Jewish movement.

There has been an ongoing debate among scholars over the existence of the historical Jesus. Recently, it has escalated with New Testament scholar, Bart Ehrman, at the center of the storm. In his recent book, Did Jesus Exist?,[54] the author departs from his usual scholarly work by participating in a public debate with Mythicist, Acharya S.D.M. Murdock, author of *The Christ Conspiracy, The Greatest Story Ever Sold.*[55] The Mythicists believe that the early church created the man, Jesus, out of the myths from the ancient past. Although I believe that these myths helped define the Jesus that took form and was canonized at the Council of Nicaea, I believe that Jesus really did exist, although he is elusive as a historical figure. Jesus was not the creation of the widespread mythology of dying and rising gods known throughout the pagan world, but the story "about" him clearly shows this influence (see chapters 12 and 13). The original Jesus, identified by his teachings, is not a myth. The tales that were created about him appear to carry strong evidence that would imply a mythological etiology found in "Christianism."

It is this "original" Jesus that this book seeks to re-discover. Hopefully, I will contribute to liberating Jesus from 2000 years of captivity within a system that bears his name. How his name became so revered and his message so distorted is the story of nineteen centuries of intentional malfeasance by the church power structure and/or unintentional misunderstanding by many well-meaning clergymen and scholars.

It is important to know the history of the development of Jesus' nature as interpreted by the church. The terms human and divine are like two poles on a continuum, yet they are part of the same whole. You can actually watch the theistic interpretation of Jesus growing as the story develops. The very early sources of the Jesus material indicate that Jesus was not a visiting deity, not an incarnation of a super-natural God, and not even a miracle worker. The supernatural suit of armor attached to Jesus was not original to the early understanding of who Jesus was.

I will briefly examine three interpretations, starting with the Adoptionists. These were the Christians who claimed that Jesus was so fully human that he could not be divine. This group maintained that Jesus was not divine, but a full, flesh-and-blood human being whom God had "adopted" to be his son, usually at his baptism. The best known adoptionistic Christians were the Ebionites (for the best in depth look at the Ebionites, look at Keith Aker's *The Lost Religion of Christianity.*). Based on their strict monotheistic belief system, the Ebionites insisted that Jesus was not himself divine, but was a human being no different in "nature" from the rest of us. They saw him as a special, righteous man, whom God had chosen and placed in a special relationship to him. The Docetics had a different Christology, claiming that Jesus just seemed to be a man, a kind of charade in which he played a human role. The Greek word *dokeo* means to appear or seem to be. The best known Docetic teacher was Marcion, against whom Irenaeus and Tertullian wrote apologies. The third group divided Jesus Christ into two: the man, Jesus (who was completely human) and the divine Christ (who was completely divine). According to this view, the man Jesus was temporarily indwelt by the divine being, Christ, enabling him to perform his miracles and deliver his teachings, but before his death, the Christ abandoned him, forcing him to face his crucifixion alone.[56]

Since Paul did not have access to the Synoptic Gospels, he knew very little about the Jesus as portrayed in these Gospels. Paul used the metaphor of adoption to describe the relationship of the Christian to God. He drew his language from the Roman law of adoption. Here are some quotes from Paul: "You have received the spirit of adoption."[57] "Jesus Christ has redeemed us that we may receive adoption as sons."[58] He did not use the term the way the Ebionites used it, but the idea is the same. In Paul we find little of the theistic framework and little of the imposed supernaturalism that was to develop later. As we have pointed out, Paul does not embrace an incarnational and Trinitarian language of a developed theism that later emerged.

Mark, the first gospel writer, describes Jesus as a God-Presence, a human being infused with God's spirit rather than a theistic deity masquerading as a human being. Mark had clearly never heard of the miraculous-birth tradition. Mark's gospel ends with the enigmatic statement that the women fled the resurrection scene in fear and said "nothing to anyone." Mark's Jesus had not been fully captured by the theistic definitions of God that later developed. Mark has Peter confessing that Jesus is the Christ, the Messiah, a God presence.[59] The earliest witnesses to Jesus (Paul, perhaps Q, Thomas, and even Mark) portrayed a Jesus whose life has not yet been squeezed into the theistic mold. Instead, Jesus is one in whom and through whom God is seen. We have a delicate task, one that walks the path between distinctions of separating the experience of religion from the explanation of that experience. In the earliest records, we find that Jesus is not pictured as a total theistic distortion as he is later portrayed by the church.

It seems that it is Matthew and Luke who bring the theistic interpretation to the life of Jesus. The Jesus depicted in Matthew's narrative is no longer quite human. He maintains that at his birth, Jesus was the incarnation of a theistic deity. The theistic understanding of God (God as external, supernatural, and invasive) is clearly the God-definition through which Matthew and Luke interpret Jesus. The writer John moves at warp speed in this direction and takes the divinity of Jesus to a new level. John appears to dismiss the virgin birth story as an inadequate explanation for the God-presence met in Jesus.

Jesus' humanity faded with each evolutionary step, while his divinity and ultimately his deity increased. Under John, theism's capture of this new faith system was complete. As theology developed in the West, Jesus became first the divine Son of God, then the incarnation of the holy God, and finally the second person of the Trinity. Theism had effectively captured Jesus and wrapped him in the garments of supernaturalism. Defense after defense was erected by the early church to protect this image of Jesus; e.g., postpartum virginity, a dogma of the Roman Catholic Church which insisted that Jesus came through the womb without breaking the hymen. This dogma totally disregards the evidence that Mary had other children.[60] I suppose some would say that she adopted them, a practice that was prevalent in the Greco-Roman world, but unheard of in Judaism.

Jesus was a spiritual mentor. Unique as a spirit person, Jesus demonstrated the subordination of subject-object reality, which creates separation by emphasizing the transpersonal, unity paradigm, at its most radical expression. His experience was noetic (subjective understanding), involving not simply a feeling of ecstasy, but a knowingness that comes from intuition. Judaism had a number of spirit people including Moses, Elijah and Enoch, to name a few. Enoch is described as having "walked with God." Jesus used spiritual practices, including fasting and prayer. Jesus' use of the word *Abba* expresses his own intimacy with an experiential reality of God. The image of God that goes with the understanding of Jesus as a spirit person is very different from the popular view. Rather than being an article of belief, God becomes an experiential reality. The Jewish tradition of which Jesus was a part, spoke of knowing God, which is the same phrase for sexual intercourse. In this context, God is not seen as a transcendent reality, but as One in whom we live and move and have our being. The view of Jesus that I have sketched shifts our focus of the Christian life from believing in Jesus or believing theological statements about him, to being in relationship with the same Spirit that Jesus knew. It moves beyond believing in God and emphasizes being in relationship with God.

Finding the real Jesus is the basis for a restored Christianity. This book calls for a rediscovery of the teachings of Jesus; and if we see Jesus primarily as a teacher, then it is important to understand what he taught. What did Jesus teach? It is a single focused message about the Kingdom of Heaven. This theme is found 13 times in Mark, 28 times in Luke and 38 times in Matthew. John uses an equivalent term, eternal life, which has much the same meaning. Jesus locates the kingdom of heaven within you.[61] The kingdom of heaven is not something coming upon us from outside ourselves. Heaven is a reality within us. Heaven is the very foundation of our personal existence and something that could be experienced by the individual. Jesus called it a mystery since it could be acquired only through individual insight and experience. The images that he used to describe the kingdom were growth images (mustard seed and leaven in the loaf).[62] For those who refused to grow, he used a metaphor of grass that is cut down and withers. Because the kingdom is associated with the inner growth of the individual, it is very much a here and now experience. The kingdom of heaven involves radical transformation as represented by the image of rebirth. It is the inward man that is capable of rebirth. This kingdom requires a new morality which is not based on rules and regulations, but one that confronts the shadowy self within us who has made all the rules and regulations necessary in the first place. This requires self-confrontation that leads to commitment to the inner way of the kingdom and to the realization that the kingdom of God is a process, a journey, a work of a lifetime. In other words, the kingdom of heaven is a spiritual reality. Jesus knew that the Spirit in man was a miracle-working power. He also knew that we do not experience this power because we make it too hard for the Spirit to express. We measure man's possibilities by his past experiences rather than by his innate potentiality. We have a choice.

Did Jesus have a theology? In the sense that theology means the study of God, then Jesus' main focus was this study. So, he did have a theology. The parable of the prodigal son is the most popular and revealing of Jesus' teachings and it is the centerpiece of his theology. It presents the condition of man and the response of God to that condition. In this parable man is not presented as a wretched sinner. He is pictured as a wayward son. God is not presented as a wrathful sovereign; He is presented as a loving Father. It is important to realize that humanity, in this parable, is not represented as being separate from God, nor is there a need of an atoning salvation.

The young prodigal son has the center stage in the first part of this drama-filled metaphor. Here we see the catastrophic fall of a man who was hell-bent on plumbing every corner of the far country. The younger son is a roguish, pleasure-seeking spendthrift. The second part of this parable finds the elder brother on center stage, but this son is dull and humdrum compared to his younger brother. This is a prodigal at heart who has learned to play it safe. This man never took risks. He may have stayed respectable only because he lacked the spirit to do anything else. The older son is duty-bound, self-righteous, unforgiving, and joyless. He was unable to understand this dramatic change of his brother, because he was viewing this change from the outside. Most of us know that there are certain truths which simply cannot be understood, but which must be experienced. The father was able to see the prodigal son from the inside, but he was also able to see the life of the elder brother from the inside, from the point of the heart. He was able to say to him, "You are my beloved son, you are always with me, and therefore we share everything."

James Weldon Johnson, a black poet from the early part of the twentieth century, has written a series of poems about Bible stories. These poems are compiled in a book, *God's Trombones*. One of the outstanding poems in this book is about this story of the prodigal son. I love the way that he introduces this poem. "Young man, young man, your arms are too short to box with God...And Jesus didn't give this man a name because this young man is every young man everywhere."[63]

Taken as outer figures, these two sons refer to two types of people: the pleasure-seeking and the super-responsible. However, when taken as inner figures, the two brothers represent two sides of one whole person. Each of us has a Pharisaic elder-brother and a wayward prodigal son side. It is this self-confrontation that leads to a commitment to the inner way of the kingdom and to the realization that the kingdom of God is a process, a journey, a work of life. Those who would achieve this kingdom must be resolutely committed to the inner work. "Once the hand is laid on the plough, no one who looks back is fit for the kingdom of God."[64] Some people come to the hard work of self-confrontation only under painful duress. When this pain is alleviated, they drop the process, revealing that they are not yet ready for kingdom work. When you really start this inner work, you could not stop it even if you wanted to. With these people, there is no longer any question of dropping the plough and turning back. The elder brother, who represents the Pharisee in us, wants to play it safe and he does so by remaining at a distance from both his Father and his brother. He is not emotionally involved with life. It is always the task of the ego to become conscious, and this can happen only as we are willing to look within and recognize our inner adversary. This always involves self-confrontation. It is interesting to note that the elder brother does not even admit to his relationship with his brother when he referred to the prodigal as "this thy son."[65]

Forgiveness is the theme of this parable; but, contrary to popular interpretation, God is not forgiving anyone of anything. God does not forgive; He is forgiveness, just as God is love. Can electricity stop being electricity? Can light stop being light? Can gravity be less than gravity? How can I get the forgiveness of electricity for disrupting its flow? It is accomplished by turning on the switch. How can I get the life force in my body to forgive me for shutting off its flow with a rubber band? I must remove the rubber band. And no one can do it for me. And the force that surges through the finger and the switch—is it forgiving me? In a way you could say that it is. But all it is really doing is being what it is. The moment I release my bitterness, rise above my guilt and stop feeling sorry for myself, in that moment the forgiveness of God sweeps through me and lifts me beyond myself. But it remains what it has always been. I have to accept it.

Power is a key to understanding forgiveness. If I resent someone, that person has some power over me; but when I forgive, I reclaim the power that bully stole from me. Thus, forgiveness benefits first and foremost the person doing the forgiving. Setting others free means setting you free because resentment is really a form of attachment. It is a Cosmic Truth that it takes two to make a prisoner—the prisoner and a jailer. Elizabeth Sand Turner writes about this parable in her book, *Your Hope of Glory*. Listen to her comments on this parable:

"The younger son symbolizes the person who has not yet been awakened to his spiritual nature and who takes his inheritance (divine substance) from his father (God) and departs into a 'far country' (material consciousness).... Because he is innately spiritual, he gradually awakens to his true nature (the prodigal son came to himself) and realizes that happiness and fulfillment can come only by a reunion with God (I will arise and go to my father)."[66]

We can use a battering ram or we can use a key to open the doors to our future good. Quite often we wish to take the kingdom by storming it. This kingdom is an inner reality that is old, yet ever new. The concept of the great within has inspired philosophers, poets and mystic teachers throughout all the ages. None has put it more eloquently than Robert Browning in his poem, "Paracelsus"[67]

Truth is within ourselves; it takes no rise
From outward things, whate'er you may believe.
There is an inmost center in us all,
Where truth abides in fullness; and around,
Wall upon wall, the gross flesh hems it in,
This perfect, clear perception which is truth.
A baffling and perverting carnal mesh
Binds it, and makes all error; and to know
Rather consist in opening out a way
Whence the imprisoned splendor may escape,
Than in effecting entry for a light, supposed to be without.

---

# Chapter 5
# WILL THE REAL PAUL STAND UP!

"There is a principle which is a bar against all information, which is proof against all argument and cannot help but keep man in everlasting ignorance, which is condemnation without investigation." Spencer, the English poet

One writer was so frustrated with the Apostle Paul that he wrote these words, "Peale is appealing, but Paul is appalling."[68] Most scholars agree; Paul is an enigma. He uses language that identifies him with the literalists and exclusivists. Yet, his experience on the Damascus road was a classical mystical encounter. I quote extensively from him, using his language to support my call for a trans-personal religious experience and yet I charge him as a co-conspirator with the bishops of Nicaea in subverting the original teachings of Jesus. I have to admit that I am confused as to the identity of the "real" Paul found in the pages of the New Testament. Could it be that we have two Pauls presented in this document? One is the Paul who presents a picture of the Mythic Christ, echoing the message found in ancient Pagan myths. The other is the orthodox Paul who preaches an exclusive, narrow, misogynistic and belief-based Christianity. It is this Paul who is the bastion of Literalistic orthodoxy. Could it be that the "real" Paul was hijacked by his disciples and converted into something that he was not? Some liberal scholars dismiss almost half of Paul's letters as forgeries, meaning that they were probably written by someone else, using Paul's name for validity.

When Paul writes about the secret of Christianity, it has nothing to do with an historical Jesus. In fact, Paul seemed to know very little about this Jesus. He never quotes Jesus and never mentions any details about his life. The life of Jesus appears to exist between the dash that separates his birth and death. This same observation is true for the Apostle's Creed. Since Paul's letters are the earliest Christian documents, predating the gospels by several decades, his account should be full of stories about the life of Jesus. He never refers to Jesus' miraculous birth. His only mention of his birth was the terse, "born of woman."[69] There is no mention of any miracles. There is no Sermon on the Mount or Lord's Prayer. There is no agony in Gethsemane, no trial, no crown of thorns, no thieves crucified with Jesus, nothing about the time and place of his execution and no Judas or Pilate. One wonders about the absence of details about this Jesus, whom he calls "Lord." Is it conceivable that Paul would have talked about the Jesus found in the Synoptic Gospels, had he known of one? He does develop a theology about the events of his death and resurrection. As a result, fundamental Christianity sees the gospel through a Pauline lens. Paul's writing is the subject of most Protestant preaching.

Paul implies that the real secret of Christianity is found in the phrase, "Christ in you, your hope of glory."[70] This phrase is Gnostic in its symbolism and represents the hero of an initiation myth. "It is no longer I who live, but Christ who lives within me"[71] is a theme echoed many times in Paul's writing.[72] But the question arises, which Paul? This is certainly not the Paul of fundamentalism and literalism.

Of the thirteen letters attributed to Paul, three of these are known as Pastoral letters and are dismissed by liberal scholars as forgeries. They are called pastoral because they provide rules for guiding the organization of the early church. These letters reflect the growth of the church as an institution that existed in the second century and not the first century when Paul wrote his original letters. Other letters are brought into serious scrutiny by scholars who question their content or their internal consistency. Most scholars will tell you that whereas seven of the thirteen letters that go under Paul's name are his, the other six are not.

The New Testament scholar, Bart Ehrman, does not shy away from using the word "lie" to describe the pseudepigraphas[73] found in the New Testament, especially in works ascribed to the Apostle Paul. Here are his strong words from his latest book, "It may be one of the greatest ironies of the Christian scriptures that some of them insist on truth, while telling a lie..... Many of the books of the New Testament were written by people who lied about their identity, claiming to be a famous apostle—Peter, Paul or James—knowing full well they were someone else. In modern parlance, that is a lie, and a book written by someone who lies about his identity is a forgery."[74]

This comment goes to the heart of the question, "Who is the real Paul?" Most scholars accept the conclusion that Paul did not write Hebrews. Authors, Marcus Borg and John Dominic Crossan, hypothesize that there are three different Pauls found in the New Testament,[75] not just two as I have suggested. These writers identify the "Real" Paul the "Radical" Paul. The "Real" Paul is revealed in his call for Philemon to free his slave, Onesimus.[76] This sounds very much like something the "Radical Jesus" would have done. This Paul wrote about the equality of men and women in Romans and the letters to the Corinthians. Borg and Crossan also believe that the "Real" Paul wrote Galatians, the Philippians and I Thessalonians. The second Paul is called "Conservative" Paul because he upholds the status quo. This Paul, they contend, wrote Colossians, Ephesians and 2 Thessalonians. The third was the "Reactionary" Paul. This is the Paul that has been branded as one of history's great misogynists. In I Timothy the writer told women to be silent in the church and to be submissive to their husbands. He reminded his readers about what happened the first time a woman was allowed to exercise authority over a man (the Garden of Eden story). He concluded that if a woman wanted to be saved, they were to have babies.[77] The problem here is that the real Paul may have never said those words attributed to him. If not, then this condemnation of Paul is a great miscarriage of literary justice.

I may have been too hard on Paul charging him with betraying the teachings of Jesus, since there are serious questions about which Paul I have leveled my condemnation against. When one embraces the fact that the writers of such books as 2 Peter, I Timothy and Ephesians felt justified to lie in order to tell the truth, the full impact of the title of my book begins to dawn on the reader.

# Chapter 6
# JESUS TAUGHT INNATE DIVINITY

"Man is the only creature who refuses to be what he is."
Albert Camus

If you believe in and practice innate divinity, it is impossible to harm another human being. This is a profound statement, but one that merits our consideration. Innate divinity means that every person is a Child of God, by merit of nothing. This is what Jesus taught and this is why his teachings have been abandoned by "Christianism." This philosophy, if implemented, would eliminate aggressive and pre-emptive wars immediately. The lyrics of a song written by Bill Provost express this Christ-centered idea succinctly:

> I behold the Christ in you, here the life of God I see, I can see a great peace, and too, I can see you whole and free. I behold the Christ in you; I can see this as you walk. I see this in all you do, I can see this as you talk, I behold God's love expressed, I can see you filled with power, I can see you ever blessed, see Christ in you hour by hour, I behold the Christ in you, I can see that perfect One, Led by God in all you do, I can see God's work is done.[78]

World peace will only occur when innate divinity is made central to the teachings of Jesus. Scriptures back this claim. The Sermon on the Mount and other verses of the New Testament substantiate this assertion. I begin with the audacious identification found in John 10:34, that the

Pharisees of Jesus' day called blasphemy. In this passage Jesus has announced his divinity by proclaiming, "I and the Father are one."[79] When confronted with this blasphemy charge, Jesus countered with a quote from Psalm 82[80] and used the Hebrew scripture against the fundamentalist of his day.

His reasoning was pure logic. Whether his argument was met by the Pharisees with agreement is rather doubtful, since these religious leaders did not reach their conclusions through the process of reason and logic. One cannot use reason to convince, unless reason is valued as a means to one's conclusions. The more certain we are about anything, the less likely we are to change our minds and reach a different conclusion. The more invested in our beliefs, the more we resist cognitive dissonance. This is the distressing mental state in which people find themselves doing things that don't fit with what they know, or having opinions that do not fit with other opinions they hold. The more committed we are to a belief, the harder it is to relinquish, even in the face of overwhelming contradictory evidence.

I agree with Paul Smith who concluded that "The greatest block to our spiritual growth is the belief that Jesus is the totally unique and only Son of God."[81] I start my scripture analysis with reference to a verse that the fundamentalist community has completely ignored or hold to a vastly different interpretation. Jesus had just finished making a "blasphemous claim." He was claiming to be divine. Then, he continued by claiming that humanity was divine. Jesus reminded the literalists to whom he was speaking that scripture cannot be annulled. Here are his shocking words,

> Is it not written in your law, "I said, you are gods?" If those to whom the word of God came were called "gods"—and the scripture cannot be annulled—can you say that the one whom God has sanctified and sent into the world is blaspheming because I said, "I am the Child of god"?[82]

It is clear that this passage is about divinity—his and ours. Why would he make such a formidable challenge as to say, "Whosoever believes in me will do the works that I do and even greater ones"?[83] I was taught that this was not possible. If not, then why did he say it? Notice that this belief in Jesus is tied to "walking the path that he walked." It has nothing to do with accepting a belief system, based on being a sinner. I love the phrase used by Paul Smith when he referred to our evolving spiritual being in his book as "baby divinities."[84] This phrase implies spiritual evolution which is the crux of spiritual growth. We don't become something that we are not as a result of some magical incantation. We become more of what we were created to be through the process of conscious growth.

It may have been appropriate for me to start with the image of God in man concept as recorded in the Book of Genesis. We are made in the image and likeness of God. "Then God said, 'Let us make humankind in our image, according to our likeness.'"[85] What part of us is like God? It certainly is not the ego self, who loves "playing God." It is obviously the "real self" or the authentic self that is made in God's image. Again, I refer to Smith's analysis of the Garden of Eden experience and the so-called "fall of man."

Somewhere deep inside each of us we are the spitting image of God! But Genesis doesn't leave that idea alone. Next, it predicts that we could actually become even "more" like god. The serpent said to Eve that if she ate of the fruit of the tree of good and evil, "your eyes will be opened and you will be like god, knowing good and evil (3:5). Of course, they were already like God but did not know it because their spiritual eyes were not yet open. Therefore, rather than a bad thing, awakening to the knowledge of good and evil was exactly what needed to happen if we were going to develop spiritually. We cannot evolve if our eyes are shut. People who do not know the difference between good and evil are considered sociopaths today. A basic facet of spiritual development is the growing ability to discern what is good from what is evil, what is loving from what is not. In effect, the serpent said, "You will awaken and you will discover that, indeed, you are divine like God." We have been taught that the serpent was lying, and it was deceiving Eve. But the serpent was actually telling the truth!...Yes folks, Genesis graphically tells the story of both biological and spiritual evolution.[86]

This passage tells us that we are intrinsically divine. God did warn us that there would be pain in our growth and so often the pain keeps us from growing. Even the Messianic child of Isaiah chapter 7 would learn the difference between good and evil as a part of his maturation process.[87] If this passage refers to Jesus, as some contend, then it implies growth and understanding as part of his development. This is a far cry from a "God with us" theology. This passage also tells us about how much growth we need to achieve. It requires a lifetime (and more).

One does not have to hold a particular doctrine, believe a particular religion or philosophy, or have a particular spiritual orientation to profit from Jesus' teachings. This is what makes these teachings universal. Jesus identifies the kingdom of heaven as within the individual.[88] Many of his parables are about growth of something from within, such as the seed or the leaven in the loaf. These images picture the evolution of the spirit as sure as new wine expands the leather cask in which it is contained. Jesus used a powerful light image when he proclaimed that he was the light of the world, which fits well with orthodox theology.[89] He then proceeds to say that, "You are the light of the world, which has never been taken seriously by his followers."[90] Another place we are told that a good tree cannot bear bad fruit and a bad tree cannot bear good fruit.[91] The entire world is a fruit inspector.

We are in essence divine beings. It is important as to how we treat one another, including our enemies. This observation usually sets the fundamentalist into a defensive mode, since Christian America has not done a very effective job of treating enemies. Have our recent wars managed to "keep us safe?" Have they "spread democracy around the world"? Usually silence or a weak protest is the answer. If something is not working, then stop doing it. To continue is the definition of insanity. Jesus said, "If you have done it to the least of these, you have done it to me," which suggests that we start treating everyone in the light of this divinity. When we do so, we are honoring Jesus.

Jesus' prayer in the Gospel of John is a call for unity or oneness. Jesus prayed, "As you, Father, are one in me and I in you, may thee also be in us...so that they be one, as we are one, I am in them and you are in me."[92] This is his reminder that we are divine. Matthew Fox reminds us that some early theologians of the church understood and wrote about this insight. He includes Athanasius, Maximus and Thomas Aquinas in his observation, maintaining that they believed and taught innate divinity.[93] When Jefferson used the phrase, "Unalienable rights," he was implying that you cannot place a lien against those rights, because they are innate.

What does the writer of I John mean when he says, "We will be like him?"[94] Since traditional Christianity cannot tolerate the divinity of humanity, this verse poses a serious problem for their theological position. Even the apostle Paul presents a mixed message when he concludes that we will be changed into the same image as Jesus.[95] I suppose he means that salvation is the agent of that change, but his use of the word "image" is reminiscent of the Genesis account of innate divinity. What does he mean when he uses "being in Christ" terminology? Knowing his theological position, I am sure he would exclude anyone who has "not been saved by the blood of Jesus." I believe that Paul did not accept Jesus' concept of innate divinity, otherwise we would not have corrupted the teaching of Jesus by his salvation theology. The two positions are incompatible.

If Jesus is the only Son of God, as fundamentalism claims, then the New Testament is wrong in calling us Sons (and Daughters) of God. Why did Jesus call himself, the "son of man," 82 times in the New Testament much more often than the phrase, "Son of God?" The writer of Hebrews says, "He was like us in every respect."[96] What does this mean? Does it mean that he just appeared to be like us, as the Docetic Christians claimed? Was he just playing a role? Or, does it really mean what it says? The Creed got it right in one important point. It claims that Jesus was fully human and fully divine, just as we are fully human and fully divine.

Several authors have used a metaphor for God and man's divinity as seen through the science of fractal images. The mathematician, Benoit Mandelbrot, describes geometric fractals as "a rough or fragmented geometric shape that can be split into parts, each of which is (at least approximately) a reduced size copy of the whole."[97] God is the whole; man is the approximate reduced size copy of that reality (the image). Smith sums it up, "Putting Jesus' words into fractal terminology, Jesus says: 'I am an exact fractal of God. I am a reduced-size copy of the whole. God is the whole. I am the fractal. You, also, are all fractals of God."[98]

The subtitle of my book contains the phrase, "Religious Truths." This teaching of Jesus about innate divinity, which has been abandoned by the church, is the greatest truth known to mankind. If you abandon this truth, you discount Jefferson's "Unalienable rights." It may be that the church has contributed to the constitutional collapse that we have witnessed in recent years by its failure to embrace innate divinity. If we would recapture this truth, we could change the world for the better. If you want a theology that takes the best of the Bible and mixes it with the best of anthropology, you will embrace this teaching. In this teaching we find "Christ in you," our hope of glory.

Let us return to the idyllic garden of Paradise. The tree of life is not forbidden, only guarded against those of us who do not yet understand how to enter its gate. Jesus' knowledge and teachings opened that gate. We are now ready to complete our journey of the development of consciousness into that garden. The kingdom of heaven is not an impossible dream in an unattainable realm, but a state of consciousness closer to us than our own breath! It has always been there for our taking by the slow, steady development of our hearts and minds. The kingdom of heaven is within us. Through Jesus' teachings, the heaven on earth will come as a present reality, when we are ready for it and are willing to pay the price to achieve it.

# Chapter 7
# JESUS AS AN ARCHETYPE

"I never will by any word or act, bow to the shrine of intolerance. I never had an opinion in politics or religion which I was afraid to own; a reserve on these subjects might have procured me more esteem from some people, but less from myself."
Source: Thomas Jefferson, The Freethinker

The image of the Pre-Easter Jesus as one who experienced God is quite different from the common understanding of Jesus. This view undermines the Christian claim that Jesus was unique and that Christianity is rightfully based on an exclusive revelation of God. The validity of his life underscores the fact that Jesus was a man for whom God was an experiential reality. God is not an article of belief; God is an experiential reality. The pre-Easter Jesus becomes a powerful testimony to the reality and know-ability of God. This understanding of Jesus shifts the focus of the Christian life from believing in Jesus or believing in God to being in a relationship with the same Spirit that Jesus knew.

"Christ" is not a person; it is a title. It is the Greek translation of the Hebrew word, Messiah or anointed of God. It is a degree of stature that Jesus attained. Because of a lifelong conditioning, most of us think of "Christ" and "Jesus" as synonymous. This distinction is the hinge upon which the whole Gospel message turns. As a powerful God Presence, Jesus defines the Divinity of Man. He discovered his own divinity, his unique relationship with the Infinite. Let me clearly state that he is not God in the ultimate sense of the word. The reason I can say that is because he said that about himself. "Don't call me good (God) there is none good but God."[99] Jesus is our "Way Shower." He has clearly blazed a trail for us. His teachings serve as a guidepost that leads us past the obstacles, which we encounter along the path. His teachings will not only keep you moving in the right direction, they will arm you with powerful tools with which you can overcome the world. Charles Fillmore, one of the great spiritual giants of the 20th century, had this to say about Jesus:

> He was more than Jesus of Nazareth, more than any other man who ever lived on earth. He was more than man, as we understand that appellation in its everyday use, because there came into His manhood a factor to which most men are strangers. This factor was the Christ consciousness. The unfoldment of this consciousness by Jesus make Him God incarnate, because Christ is the Mind of God individualized. We cannot separate Jesus Christ from God or tell where man leaves off and God begins in Him. To say that we are men as Jesus was a man is not exactly true, because, He had dropped that personal consciousness by which we separate ourselves from our true God self . . He became consciously one with the absolute principle of Being. He proved in His resurrection and ascension that He had no consciousness separate from that of Being; therefore He was this Being to all intent and purpose. Yet He attained no more than what is expected of every one of us.[100]

The above quote is a perfect description of our highest transpersonal state. Moving onward in your quest for spiritual transformation, you will discover Jesus' teachings ever waiting for you like familiar ribbons tied to trees, letting you know you are on the right trail and leading you higher and higher in your awareness of God. The teachings of your Master Trailblazer about the nature of God and the kingdom of heaven as well as His principles of healing and love have been thoughtfully and lovingly placed before you so that you will always know that you are not alone. The teachings of Jesus Christ stand alone; they need no accoutrements. Without any involvement with Him personally, they are entirely sufficient to help you be the person you were created to be. In fact, His teachings can (and were meant to) transform the entire world. That was and is their purpose: to bring to all humanity the news that we are part of God and that God's desire for each of us is absolute good.

Emilie Cady, a new-thought writer, helps us bring the idea of the Christ into the transpersonal context, which lies within, when she writes:

> We all must recognize that it was the Christ within which made Jesus what He was; and our power now to help ourselves and to help others, lies in our comprehending the Truth—for it is a Truth whether we realize it or not—that this same Christ lives within us, which ever lives there, with an inexpressible love and desire to spring to the circumference of our being, or to our consciousness, as our sufficiency in all things.[101]

In your personal quest, you may be making the same discoveries that Jesus made; and if you are, you will be having the exhilarating experience of realizing your life is getting better and better all the time. More than ever before, you will be able to handle whatever is yours to handle as you increasingly understand that you have a power within you which makes all things possible. To be sure, the teachings of Jesus Christ are, in a very real sense, lifesaving, "miracle working" revelations. We join with you in sincere gratitude for them and for Him for sharing His quest with us.

Not everyone who follows these universal teachings is interested in knowing the Teacher, but maybe you, like me, desire to know Jesus Christ better. Knowing His beautiful teachings, perhaps you now crave a personal relationship with Him who revealed them. How can you achieve this desire, since he has been gone over 2000 years? Followers through the centuries claim to have had a mystical experience of his presence. How this can happen and what this means is a major quest for the seeker. The consciousness of Jesus the Christ has never left our world. This is explained best in terms of an archetype. The contemporary Jesus is not a person; he is an archetype. He is a combination of fact and myth. Were the historical Jesus to return to this earth today, we would not recognize him.

Archetype is a word of which you may never have heard. Carl Jung was the first to define and explore the nature and role of universal archetypes in human consciousness. By their very nature, Jung explained, archetypes have their origins in the dawn of human history. Jung tied archetypes inextricably to his concept of the collective unconscious, which is distinct from the individual unconscious. The collective unconscious is the inherited experience of the entire human race. Your consciousness is affected by this greater unconscious, and your consciousness makes a contribution to the collective consciousness. Echoing Plato, Jung defined archetypes as definite forms in the psyche that seem to be present always and everywhere. Although archetypes are patterns of influence that are both ancient and universal, they become quite personalized when they are a part of an individual's own psyche. An archetype gains strength and energy the longer it exists. The present consciousness of Jesus is greater now than when he was alive. His influence took on a greater dimension the moment he died. The Post Resurrection Jesus was certainly not the Jesus of pre Crucifixion. The moment he died, the myths began to grow. They grew because he touched a resonant chord of truth in every follower. Their additions were not fairy tales; they were the natural perceptions of a person who saw in the life and ministry of Jesus a truth that transcended facts. That is the real definition of the word "myth". In the flesh he was limited to time and space constraints. He could not be in two places at once. Now his spirit and the love that conveyed his presence became available to his followers on a constant basis. They felt free to create stories that expressed what he meant to them personally and individually, which is the essence of a myth.

Alvin Boyd Kuhn summarizes the archetype motif in the following observation: "If the Occident loses the physiological uplift of its humanized divine archetype, it will gain in its place the archetype of an everlasting, ever dynamic ideal reality. And just as an anthropomorphic deity has lost its hold on the modern mind, so will the canonized personage of history yield to the more universal and durable ideal archetype of Spiritual Man, the full realization of the human potential that is of divine origin—the Christ within the heart."[102]

The Jesus archetype continues to grow today. There are writers who claim to channel Jesus. Storytellers feel free to create a yarn about Jesus' travel in India and Egypt. Recent volumes have been written which claim to be the revelation of Jesus Christ. There is no difference, in my opinion, between these accounts and the ones that followed his death, only a time dimension. If they speak the truth of his teachings, they have validity, especially if they center on the Love motif. Most popular among these new revelations is the work of Esther Hicks (born Esther Weaver), an American inspirational speaker and best-selling author. She has co-authored nine books with her husband Jerry Hicks. They present workshops on "The Law of Attraction" and appear in the first release of the film, *The Secret*. The Hicks' books, including the best-selling series, *The Law of Attraction*,[103] have broad appeal among New Thought readers.

Is it possible to connect with the historical Jesus? Schweitzer tried it and felt his efforts were futile. This does not mean that Schweitzer denied the existence of the historical Jesus. He believed that the effort to search for him in the historical documents is doomed to failure. The popular image of Jesus, which is archetypal in nature, is quite different from the original image, which reflected his own self-understanding. Did Jesus think and speak of himself as the Son of God whose historical intention or purpose was to die for the sins of the world? I think not. Was his message about believing in him or believing him and his teachings? The latter image leads to a different image of the Christian life. The emphasis on Jesus' teaching and the gospels, as a way or path, points to an understanding of the religious life as a journey. These are seen in the great stories of the Bible: the Exodus, the exile and return.

Bishop Spong[104] points out that the priestly story produces severe distortions in our understanding of the Christian life.

- It leads to a static understanding of the Christian life.
- It creates a passive understanding of the Christian life. (The priestly story is culturally domesticating, while the stories of Egypt and Babylon are culturally subversive.)
- It leads to an understanding of Christianity as primarily a religion of the afterlife.
- God becomes primarily the lawgiver and judge. (God does for us what we cannot do for ourselves and his forgiveness becomes conditional.) The priestly story places the grace of God within a system of requirements.
- This story is very hard to believe. The notion that God's only son came to this planet to offer his life as a sacrifice for the sins of the world, and that God could not forgive us without that having happened, and that we are saved by believing this story, is simply incredible.
- For some (without a sense of guilt) this story has nothing to say.

The New Testament has its own journey story. It is the story of discipleship. The meaning of the word disciple is the initial clue. It does not mean to be a student of a teacher, but rather to be a follower of somebody. Discipleship in the New Testament is submitting to the discipline and teaching of Jesus, a journeying with him. Undisciplined "believers" are impostors. This is the real charge against Paul made by James and Peter. To follow Jesus means to accept the high level of consciousness that he achieved. To journey with Jesus means listening to his teachings, sometimes understanding them sometimes not quite getting them. It can involve denying him, even betraying him.

It also means seeing Jesus as the great discoverer of the Divinity of Man, the pioneer and way-shower in the great world of the within. That journey can be in his presence, as an existential reality. Journeying with Jesus means to be in a community, to become part of an alternative community of Jesus. To Jesus, religion was not simply a way of believing or worshiping, it was a way of living. It is a road less traveled, as part of a community that remembers and celebrates Jesus, not because of what he did, but because of who he was and what he taught. A traveler in ancient Greece had lost his way. Seeking to find it, he asked directions of a man by the roadside who turned out to be Socrates. "How can I reach Mt. Olympus", asked the traveler? To this Socrates is said to have replied, "Just make every step you take go in that direction." This implies that we must know that direction.

# Chapter 8
# THEY EVEN LIED ABOUT HIS NAME!

"The whole history of these books (i.e. the Gospels) is so
defective and doubtful that it seems vain to attempt minute
enquiry into it and such tricks have been played with their text."
Source: Letter of Thomas Jefferson to John Adams

Christian fundamentalists claim that all one need do is
"Call upon the name of Jesus and they will be saved." They
are ignorant of the fact that the name Jesus did not exist
before the fourteenth century. There was no J in any language prior to the 14th century. In Hebrew we know there
was no J either, so Jesus was originally spelled Yeshua. But
the ua ending in Yeshua's name, when transliterated into
Greek, is feminine singular, which presents a problem. The
Church simply changed ua to u; thus Jesus became a male
savior. What most people do not understand is that the us
ending to Jesus' name was set up to denote male gen-
der. The ous and the us ending in the Greek name Iesous
and the Latin name Ieus also denote the masculine singular. Where did the name Jesus originate? Simply put, it was
derived from the Latin Iesus, which was derived from the
Greek Iesous, which in turn was derived from the Egyptian
Iusa. The name Jesus has Egyptian roots. So I would cau-
tion my fundamentalist friends to call upon the right name
if they wish to be saved.[105]

The jump between the examination and consideration
of the evidence thus presented in this chapter and applying it to one's belief system is huge. It is a psychological leap

of logic, which is an antithetical phrase, since our belief is usually conditioned by our psychology. Leap is usually associated with faith, e.g. Kierkegaard's "leap of faith." Kierkegaard identifies faith with passion, which is an emotional response. Faith, to me, is a response of the mind as identified by the writer of Hebrews.[106] "Faith is the substance of things hoped for and the evidence of things not seen." You do not have faith; you are faith. It is one of the twelve faculties of man that Charles Fillmore talks about in his writings.

Faith, like the grain of a mustard seed that Jesus talked about in his parable, is obviously not a matter of the intellect or will; but rather, a function of the soul. We mistake faith for a belief in creedal statements. Faith is a fundamentally important element in the journey to the kingdom of heaven on which Jesus focused. When Jesus speaks about faith, he is not talking about doctrinal faith. He speaks about a certain capacity of a person to affirm life, even in the face of doubts. "Lord, I believe, help thou mine unbelief."[107] It is quite possible for our intellectual beliefs to actually get in the way of a living faith. The importance of faith is central to the teachings of Jesus about healing.[108]

# Chapter 9
# JESUSONIAN CHRISTIANITY

*In every country and in every age, the priest has been hostile to liberty. He is always in alliance with the despot, abetting his abuses in return for protection to his own. Thomas Jefferson, letter to Horatio G. Spafford, March 17, 1814*

I do not use the word "truth" lightly. I prefer to substitute the word "original," especially when defining Christianity. In the main, the original message of Jesus has been suppressed, buried, evidence destroyed, misquoted and substituted with a story far different than the one the supposed founder of Christianity initiated. I do not believe that Jesus was the founder of Christianity. In fact, he was not interested in founding another religion. He wished only to reform Judaism. The real founder of Christianity was the Apostle Paul, who presented another gospel, one that does not agree with the teachings of Jesus. My work is not an attack on Christianity, although its defenders may think so. Christianity has generated much good in the world, in spite of its self-imposed and debilitating flaws, most of which were spawned in the third century. It may be helpful to identify my particular brand of Christianity as "Jesusonian Christianity." I remain true to the teachings of Jesus and not the teachings about Jesus. After all, Paul never met Jesus and did not relate to the crux of his teachings. By this definition, Paul was not a disciple of Jesus. He created another gospel, based on original sin and a sacrificial interpretation of the Crucifixion.

What do we call ourselves, those who view the evidence about Jesus differently? Are we Christian? It all depends on what you mean by the term "Christian." If it means walking the "Roman Road"[109] then we do not qualify for that distinction. The phrase "Roman Road" is a theological path demanded by those who follow the Apostle Paul, as found in the Book of Romans. It is a series of self-depreciating assertions that include universal sinfulness, the need for confession and forgiveness, and the acceptance of vicarious atonement. I have come to recognize that I am not a traditional Christian in any sense and probably do not qualify to be called a Christian. I recommend that those who believe as I should call themselves Jesusonian Christians. This appellation recognizes that we follow the pre-Easter Jesus, not the post-Easter Jesus. The post Easter Jesus is a creation of the Church and centers on belief. It is a belief system that has taken ancient stories and imposed these stories on Jesus, while at the same time claiming that their stories are unique, original and exclusive.

This is a popular view of Jesus that is completely foreign to what Jesus thought and said about himself. These two images of Jesus today stand in juxtaposition with each other. The first is a popular image of Jesus that insists that one believe in Jesus in order to inherit eternal life. It is a belief that certain teachings about Jesus are critical and are necessary for salvation. Commitment to Christ means a commitment to certain doctrines, dogmas and political agendas of conservative Christianity. Another view is not as popular. It is an image of Jesus as teacher. This view sees Jesus as a teacher of a new morality which brings a new code of righteousness. It is living a life as Jesus lived his life. It includes the Great Commandment of love of God and love of neighbor and self. It is the Golden Rule of how to treat yourself and others. The Christian life is primarily not about believing, but it is about a relationship and a connection with God as our

Source. The Christian life is about entering into a relationship that involves one in a journey of transformation.

- Jesusonian Christianity recognizes and honors religious differences without creating division over the differences.
- Jesusonian Christianity honors people of every culture and religion without losing one's personal identity and belief system.
- Jesusonian Christianity accepts the rule of love without imposing external rules on self or other people.
- Jesusonian Christianity accepts no creed, doctrine or dogma that defines the individual as an extension of the group of which he/she is a part.

Jesus did not minimize the difference between what he taught and the teachings of the Pharisees, but he did not allow those differences to separate him from them. Jesus did not compromise his beliefs, but his beliefs did not define him. He was defined by his connection with his Source, which he called "Father". His teachings contradicted traditional Judaism, yet he tried to remain in the main stream that connected him to his heritage. He had to make a decision, to identify with the prophets or the priests, both of whom were bedrock Jews, but were totally different in orientation. There is at least one passage in the Gospels that would indicate that his teachings would create division even within one's family. It is not known whether Jesus saw his teachings as divisive or if this was an unintended consequence of those teachings. Here is the passage that has generated much controversy:

"Do not think that I came to bring peace on Earth; I did not come to bring peace, but a sword. For I came to set a man against his father, and a daughter against her mother, and a daughter-in-law against her mother-in-law; and a man's enemies will be the members of his household.

He who loves father or mother more than Me is not worthy of Me; and he who loves son or daughter more than Me is not worthy of Me. And he who does not take his cross and follow Me is not worthy of Me. He who has found his life will lose it, and he who has lost his life for My sake will find it."[110]

This passage has been identified by one writer as the Jesus nobody wants to know. There have been many interpretations of this passage ranging from advocacy of physical violence to the results of ideological conflict. I think the sword is used as a metaphor for dividing people into those who accept and those who reject Jesus' teaching. Jesus is saying that his mission on earth is not to bring about world peace; it is to teach people the way to obtain spiritual salvation. His teaching on the way to obtain spiritual salvation is like a sword because it separates people into those who believe and those who do not. Jesus is saying specifically that his teaching will cut through families like a sword, with some family members believing and following Jesus' teaching and other family members rejecting Jesus' teaching. However, the preponderance of Jesus' teachings is based on peace, love and reconciliation.

Do followers of Jesus have to abandon their personal identity and belief system in order to honor and respect the beliefs of others? I think not. What I believe is right for me; it may not be right for someone else. This distinguishes Jesusonian Christianity from rigid fundamentalism. It is O.K. to feel that I am right for me without falling into the arrogance of believing that I am ultimately right; and, therefore, you need to accept my rightness. Charles Fillmore is famous for saying that he reserved the right to change his mind, since he was a product in process.

The law of love, which is an oxymoron, predominates in Jesusonian Christianity. Rules have never worked and never will. This is the reason why Jesus came to fulfill the law, by supplanting it with a higher morality. It is an ethic of the kingdom, based on an internal control, not an outer authority based on rules. Fundamentalists fear that civilization will sink into moral anarchy without a behavior-controlling religious institution. Jesus never had such fears, since he knew that internal control was more powerful than external control. The Beatitudes are Jesus' ethical touchstone. *The Urantia Book*[111] amplifies this observation: "The Master made it clear that the kingdom of heaven must begin with, and be centered in, the dual concept of the truth of the fatherhood of God and the correlated fact of the brotherhood of man. The acceptance of such a teaching, Jesus declared, would liberate man from the age-long bondage of animal fear and at the same time enrich human living with the following endowments of the new life of spiritual liberty." One cannot be free and bound at the same time, and that is the reason why Jesusonian Christianity is so liberating; it is based on Love.

Let me reiterate. Jesusonian Christianity accepts no creed, doctrine or dogma that defines the individual as an extension of the group of which he/she is a part. This statement is the defining difference between Jesusonian Christianity and "Christianism." The followers of Jesus are not defined by the group of which they are a part; nor are they defined by the creeds, doctrines or dogmas that they hold. We all have a doctrine or a belief system, but the difference is found in the restrictive nature of those doctrines or the liberating nature of those doctrines. Jesusonian Christians are free to examine and question their doctrines without feeling guilty for that examination. In fact, the followers of Jesus are encouraged to make this examination without concern for consequences. We are not concerned about preserving a tradition or defending a faith. We seek only to determine the truth, knowing all the while that the process is as important as the destination. "You shall know the truth and the truth shall set you free" (John 8:32).

# Chapter 10
# A CARICATURE OF CHRISTIANITY

"I do not find in orthodox Christianity one redeeming feature."
Thomas Jefferson

Alvin Boyd Kuhn was the first writer to differentiate between what he called "Christianity" and "Christianism." He claims that the historical faith known as Christianity has no sound claim to the title since it's far from being true Christianity. If there is to be a restoration of true Christianity to its proper place, then this distinction is necessary according to him. This leads us to the question, "What is true Christianity?" Original Christianity was not a religious system; it was a way of life. This distinction is the difference between a religion that works and one that works at creating a system where people are controlled by either fear, intimidation, or indoctrinated beliefs.

There were two camps within Old Testament Judaism, the priests and the prophets. The prophets followed the axiom of Micah who said, "What does the Lord require of thee, but to do justice, love mercy and walk humbly with thy God."[112] Micah rejected the sacrificial system as a valid pathway to performing these tasks and as the link to knowing God. The priest, on the other hand, believed in and demanded that the Jews abide by the sacrificial system and follow the legal regimen. With which camp do you believe Jesus identified? It is obvious that he chose the prophets. He felt comfortable with the teachings of Jeremiah, Isaiah, and other Old Testament prophets, who saw God as a loving and compassionate creator. Christianity must choose either to identify with Jesus or with Paul. God is either Unconditional Love or He is not. There is no text more confusing than John 3:16-17. One moment we see God as total Love, and the next we see Him as total wrath. This does not square with the teachings of Jesus, who presented God as Unconditional Love.

Early Christianity was closer to a fraternity than it was a religion. In the early stages there was little or no organization. The rivalry between the Jewish community and the early Christians did not develop until after the crucifixion, when the developing church began to separate from its Jewish roots under the leadership of the Apostle Paul. Before the crucifixion, there was an intense rivalry between the followers of Jesus and those of John the Baptist. It is popular among scholars to claim that John the Baptist was an Essene, and there are certainly similarities between him and that group. Incidentally, the word Essene was derived from the Greek words *essaios*, meaning secret or mystic, and *essenoi*, indicating healing or physician. John the Baptist came out of the desert, where the Essenes were located, around Qumran on the shores of the Dead Sea. He, as well as they, preached a gospel of baptism unto repentance. Both John and the Essenes used Isaiah 40:3 to describe themselves as a "voice crying in the wilderness." Although those who followed John the Baptist began to diminish, there is a tiny community in Iraq called the Mandaeism. They are often called the Christians of Saint John, as he is held as a very sacred person, but not indispensable in their theology. Their name is Aramaic for 'knowledge'; i.e., a translation from the Greek *gnosis*. They are Gnostic in their theology, holding to baptism as the central facet of their faith.

Controversy and schisms seem to be common among those who followed the teachings of the Essenes' and those who followed the Hellenized teachings of the Apostle Paul. James and Mary Magdalene were at odds with

Paul, as there were immense squabbles over the minutest issue. In his Galatians epistle,[113] Paul became so upset over the controversy of circumcision that he expressed a wish that those involved in the controversy would emasculate themselves. It was not long before the Pauline side of Christianity began to castigate the original Jewish Christians as heretics. Elaine Pagels observed: "Diverse forms of Christianity flourished in the early years of the Christian movement. Hundreds of rival teachers all claimed to teach the 'true doctrine of Christ' and denounced one another as frauds. Christians in churches scattered from Asia Minor to Greece, Jerusalem, and Rome split into factions, arguing over church leadership. All claimed to represent 'the authentic tradition.'"[114]

One can see that controversy is nothing new to the church. An early group that persisted, to the chagrin of the early church leaders, was Gnosticism. Gnosticism is the teaching based on Gnosis, the knowledge of transcendence arrived at by way of interior, intuitive means. Although Gnosticism rests on personal religious experience, it is a mistake to assume all such experience results in Gnostic conclusions. It is nearer the truth to say that Gnosticism expresses a specific religious experience, an experience that does not lend itself to the language of theology or philosophy. Gnosticism seems to align with the medium of myth. Indeed, one finds that most Gnostic scriptures take the form of myths. As mentioned before, the term "myth" should not be taken to mean "stories that are not true"; but rather, that the truths embodied in these myths are of a different order from the dogmas of theology or the statements of philosophy. Simon the Magician, the founder of Gnosticism, is known as the "Father of All Heretics." He believed that because the soul exists outside the body, humans have access to universal knowledge by way of Gnosis. Since all knowledge is primitive in origin, one author claims that Christianity was a branch of Gnosticism, observing that Gnosticism is found in early Christian writings. Gnosticism can be seen as Christian existentialism since its emphasis is on experience and not explanation.

Some of my friends have labeled me Gnostic. Before I can identify with this label, let's look at an understanding of Gnosticism as attacked by early orthodox theologians and the evidence many scholars find in the Nag Hammadi Library. Probably the best work submitted by a scholar on this subject is the book written by Elaine Pagels. She speculates on the impact of these documents today, and what might have happened to them should they have been found 1000 years earlier: "When Mohammed Ali smashed that jar filled with papyrus on the cliff near Nag Hammadi and was disappointed not to find gold, he could not have imagined the implications of his accidental find. Had they been discovered 1,000 years earlier, the Gnostic texts almost certainly would have been burned for their heresy. But they remained hidden until the twentieth century, when our own cultural experience has given us a new perspective on the issues they raise. Today we read them with different eyes, not merely as 'madness and blasphemy' but as Christians in the first centuries experienced them—a powerful alternative to what we know as orthodox Christian tradition. Only now are we beginning to consider the questions with which they confront us."[115]

Drawing from her research from these documents, Pagels shows us that the early church, far from being a united body, was deeply split from its very beginning. The followers of Jesus were not in agreement, even on the facts of his life as presented in the first four gospels. We have already seen that these writers did not agree on the basic facts of Jesus' life and ministry much less the meaning of his teachings. From the Gnostic gospels, we learn the shocking news that God was referred to as both Father and Mother implying that men and women were spiritual equals.

The Gnostics were condemned as heretic by the Orthodox Church and many were tortured or burned at the stake for their belief. After being hidden for centuries, the Gnostic documents are now available for study by both the scholar and the layman. It is in the light of this body of evidence that we have been called to re-evaluate the origins and meanings of Christianity. Pagles raises the question about the nature of the church as a body of people who had found and were practicing "the truth." It is obvious that both sides believed that they had codified truth and were the purveyors of that truth. The main difference between the orthodox and the Gnostics is that the orthodox claimed to possess truth, while the Gnostic claimed only to be "seekers of truth." It is with this spirit that I can identify, since I do not believe that truth can be possessed. The Gnostics identified the church as a collection of people identified by the quality of their relationship with God and one another. This is in stark distinction to the Orthodox Church, which defines the church in terms of one's relationship to the clergy, dogma, doctrine and creeds. This is what I call "second hand Christianity." The Gnostic did not see Christianity in terms of answers, but in terms of the quality of one's questions. Their engagement in the process of seeking is what draws me to them in terms of authenticity and genuineness.

There are some problems with the Gnostic philosophy that make me hesitate to identify with this group completely, especially in their interpretation of evil. Having won the battle theologically against the Gnostics, the Church lost the battle psychologically by continuing to preach an ethic that, in effect, labeled the body as evil. Orthodox Christians have questioned the obvious intellectual and spiritual elitism of the Gnostics as being inconsistent with the concept of salvation. Why would God save only the elite few is a question that makes sense, if seen from a soteriological construct. If salvation is the issue, then this claim has merit. If, as the Gnostics claim, the purpose of religion is to release "the imprisoned splendor," then salvation is a moot issue. If man were never separate from God (by sin) then there is no need for salvation; there is only a need for enlightenment and this would require insight and effort. If man were separated by sin, then the way of salvation must of necessity be simple. Does this square with the teachings of Jesus, whom Mark declared concealed his teaching from the masses, and entrusted them only to the few, whom he considered worthy to receive it?[116]

Pagels summed it up in the conclusion of her book: "We can see, then, how conflicts arose in the formation of Christianity between those restless, inquiring people who marked out a solitary path of self-discovery and the institutional framework that gave to the great majority of people religious sanction and ethical direction for their daily lives. The concerns of Gnostic Christians survived only as a suppressed current, like a river driven underground."[117] This bubbling underground river has surfaced in our age due to the discovery of the Nag Hammadi Library. Only a person blinded by dogmatic theology can close his eyes to this evidence.

We have charged that the falsifiers of the third century turned what was originally an allegorical and spiritual message into literal history and destroyed any evidence of an interpretation that would contradict or challenge their position. They conveniently burned thousands of books that were written to substantiate the metaphorical interpretation of the life and ministry of Jesus. In the process they created a Jesus that does not resemble the man who called men to embrace their innate divinity by living a life that corresponds with that embrace.

This idea is amplified by Manly Hall.

> According to the Hebrew Cabala, Gnostics seek to know the "secrets" of God. There is some evidence that Jesus taught "secrets" to his disciples which he withheld from the public. Listen to John and Matthew:

"Jesus answered him, I spake openly to the world; I even taught in the synagogue, and in the temple, whither the Jews always resort; and in secret have I said nothing" (John 18:20). " And the disciples came, and said unto him, 'Why speakest thou unto them in parables?' He answered and said unto them, because it is given unto you to know the mysteries of the kingdom of heaven, but to them it is not given. For to him who has (knowledge) will more be given, and he will have abundance; but from him who has not, even what he has will be taken away. This is why I speak to them in parables, because seeing they did not see, and hearing, they do not hear, nor do they understand" (Matthew 13:10-11). Again in Mark 4:33 he added, "With many such parables he spoke the word to them, as they were able to hear it; he did not speak to them without a parable, but privately to his own disciples he explained everything." Manley Hall believes that Jesus and other teachers guarded their "inner knowledge" so that the profane might not abuse them. He wrote: "The entire New Testament is in fact an ingeniously concealed exposition of the secret processes of human regeneration."[118]

The Gnostics, of any age, can subscribe to the outward doctrines of any religion because they have an inner knowing that allows them to transcend the external practices of even Christianity. That is the reason why their influence is so profound today, even if we are not aware of its origins. There is a correlation between them and Freemasons, who practice their secret rituals, yet blend into their Baptist churches without any feeling of contradiction.

There are some who have suggested that Jesus was an Essene, thus Gnostic in his orientation. Manley Hall believes that Jesus' parents were members of the Qumran group, along with his brother James. Keith Akers[119] argues against this claim, asserting that Qumran is laid out like military barracks and does not square with what is known about

Essense beliefs and lifestyle. Jim Marrs has an interesting aside on Jesus' hometown of Nazareth. He draws his material from Gardner, who claims that Jesus did not come from Nazareth. He said that the word 'Nazarene' and its variants came from the Hebrew word Nozrim, a plural noun stemming from the term Nazie ha-Brit 'Keepers of the Covenant,' a designation of the Essene Community at Qumran. It is actually a point of contention whether the town of Nazareth existed at all during Jesus' lifetime.[120]

# Chapter 11
# THEY PROMOTED JESUS TO GOD

But every state, says an inquisitor, has established some religion. No two, say I have established the same. Is this a proof of the infallibility of establishments? Thomas Jefferson, Notes on the State of Virginia, 1781-82

Although what happened at the Council of Nicaea in 325 C.E. was the culmination of the developing theology within the church, orthodox theology was codified and dogmatized at this meeting attended by 225 celibate bishops. The development of the Christian religion found full expression in this democratic process. They met and voted. The group who voted for the proposal won. The group who voted against was disenfranchised. The Council was a gathering of Christian leaders, who promoted Jesus to God. This council was convened by order of Constantine, the Roman emperor. He had been a leader in the cult known as Sol Invictus (Invincible Sun) and now wanted to unite the Christian sects in the empire under his existing church, the Universal Church of Rome. Many changes to the religion of Christianity were about to take place at that council, including:

- Formulation for wording the Trinity based on Athanasius.
- Changing Verses of Bible.
- Eliminating certain verses and books from the Bible.

- Declaring Arian's Unitarian (the Unity of God) as heresy.
- Changing the day of worship from Saturday to Sunday.
- Changing the date of Jesus' birthday to December 25th..
- Introduction of Easter (pagan worship, "Feast of Ishtar").
- Church of Rome "officially" became the Universal Church.

This is the Nicene Creed of 325 C.E.:

"We believe in one God, the Father Almighty, maker of all things visible and invisible. And in one Lord Jesus Christ, the son of God, begotten of the Father (the only-begotten; that is of the essence of the Father God of God, Light of Light, very God of very God, begotten, not made, being of one substance with the Father; By whom all things were made (both in heaven and on earth); who for us men, and for our salvation, came down and was incarnate and was made man; He suffered, and the third day he rose again, ascended into heaven; From there he shall come to judge the quick and the dead and in the Holy Ghost." The creed of Constantinople (381) made this addition: "was incarnate of the Holy Ghost of the virgin Mary, and made man; he was crucified for us under Pontius Pilate and suffered, and was buried, the third day he rose again, according to the scriptures, and ascended into heaven and sitteth on the right hand of the Father. And in the Holy Ghost, the Lord and Giver of life, who proceedeth from the Father who with the Father and the Son together is worshiped and glorified, who spake by the prophets. In one holy catholic and apostolic church; we acknowledge one baptism for the remission of sin, we look for the resurrection of the dead, and the life of the world to come. Amen."

Notice, that there is no mention of the life and teachings of Jesus, which covered several years. According to this creed, the important events in the life of Jesus were his birth, his death and his resurrection. The major part of his life was reduced to a comma in between his birth and death. At Nicaea they created a new Jesus and a new Christianity. The controversy of the Nicaea debate greatly agitated Emperor Constantine, and he sent a letter to Arius and Alexander in an attempt to persuade them to lay aside their differences. Constantine wrote these words:

"This contention has not arisen respecting any important command of the law, nor has any new opinion been introduced with regard to the worship of God; but you both entertain the same sentiments, so that you may join in one communion. It is thought to be not only indecorous, but altogether unlawful, that so numerous a people of God should be governed and directed at your pleasure, while you are thus emulously contending with each other, and quarrelling about small and very trifling matters."[121]

Constantine did play an important role at the Council, although there is no indication that he was allowed a vote. It may be that the eloquence and glory of the Emperor had sway with some. However, it should be remembered that he did eventually (years after the Council) support the Arian party, the group that was condemned by the Nicene Council. A few years after the Council of Nicaea, Arius discovered a new way to interpret the word "homoousius" that agreed with his doctrines. He then asked to be readmitted to communion, but the Church refused. Arius then appealed to the Emperor. Emperor Constantine's favorite sister, Constantia, on her deathbed, implored Constantine to support Arius and he did so.

Socrates Scholasticus (a detractor of Arius) described Arius's death as follows:
It was then Saturday, and going out of the imperial palace, attended by a crowd of Eusebian [Eusebius of Nicomedia is meant here] partisans like guards,

he [Arius] paraded proudly through the midst of the city, attracting the notice of all the people. As he approached the place called Constantine's Forum, where the column of porphyry is erected, a terror arising from the remorse of conscience seized Arius, and with the terror a violent relaxation of the bowels: he therefore enquired whether there was a convenient place near, and being directed to the back of Constantine's Forum, he hastened thither. Soon after a faintness came over him, and together with the evacuations his bowels protruded, followed by a copious hemorrhage, and the descent of the smaller intestines: moreover portions of his spleen and liver were brought off in the effusion of blood, so that he almost immediately died. The scene of this catastrophe still is shown at Constantinople, as I have said, behind the shambles in the colonnade; and by persons going by pointing the finger at the place, there is a perpetual remembrance preserved of this extraordinary kind of death.[122]

Theologians, obviously, took their guarded positions quite seriously with psychosomatic consequences. This episode gives new meaning to the phrase, "Don't get your bowels in an uproar."

The reader may need an amplification of the word, *homoousius*, which played a major role in the controversy at Nicaea. *Homoousian* is a technical theological term used in discussions of the Christian understanding of God as Trinity. The Nicene Creed describes Jesus as being *homooúsios* with God the Father; that is, they are of the "same substance" and are equally God. This term, adopted by the Council of Nicaea, was intended to add clarity to the relationship between Jesus and God the Father within the Godhead. It is my contention that this doctrine is in contradistinction to what Jesus believed about himself and the phrase that was used by the Synoptic writers to describe him as "The Son of Man". This phrase is used 82 times in the four Gospels, and is used only in the Sayings of Jesus. It only occurs four times in other New Testament books. This fact reveals the early movement away from the picture of Jesus as presented by his earliest followers, which was either "Son of Man" or "Son of God."

As we progress, the reader will notice a bit of cynicism on my part regarding the value of democracy. I will speak in detail about my objection to this process in my second volume on *Secular Lies*. Briefly, the best definition I have found for democracy is: "Two wolves and a sheep, voting what's for dinner." There were 220 men (Eusebius count) 318 men (Athanasius count) who voted and determined what was the truth at the Council of Nicaea. Yes, truth was discovered through opinions, although all invited did not get a chance to express their opinion. Although 1800 men were invited, only a few made the trip. The full truth about Christianity's rise and spread has never been fully told, mainly because it has been obscured with so many lies. "Christianism" is not (and never has been) Christianity in its original form. Some (including Emerson, Lincoln and Edison) have found this "substitute Christianity" to be repugnant to every instinct of logic. One has only to read the horrors of the church as recorded by Christian historians to realize that these records include not only the inquisitions, but practices that drove nearly half of Europe out of the Christian camp during the past century. Substitute Christianity has hypnotized the masses into believing that an honest assessment of Christianity's roots (which include its dark side) threatens the very existence of Christianity. Listen to Augustine describe the hubris of church leaders: "There are many things that are true which is not useful for the vulgar crowd to know; and certain things which although they are false it is expedient for the people to believe otherwise" (City of God). This is a blatant repudiation of truth in order to further the agenda of Substitute Christianity for the purpose of power, control and vested interest. Truth is never an enemy, for real religion needs no defense. Real Christianity is something quite different from what I see in American churches today, and I intend to point out these differences.

That the clergymen attending the Nicaea Council used the practice of voting to determine the will of God is not new. This practice has historical precedence in Judaism. The Hebrew Priests used a system that is akin to gambling. It is called the Urim and Thummin.[123] This method was the same that the disciples used to select Judas' replacement.

With added frustration, I sat down several years ago to address the culpability of preacher, priest, and scholar on the growing evidence emerging from New Testament scholarship and its challenge to the traditional Christian interpretation. I concluded, then, that there was, at best, a conspiracy of silence between the scholars and their pupils, the parish minister and priest. The latter received all the information from their Seminary that would challenge any astute student to reevaluate the position of orthodox Christianity. Yet, they returned from divinity school to preach the party line, justifying their capitulation by practical rationalizations. I realize that I have been too hard on these practitioners. They were, for the most part, speaking to and restricted by an adolescent insistence on security and the fear to examine facts that would challenge their cherished beliefs. It is interesting to watch the religious leaders use the tools that normally excavate and reveal truth, to cover up the facts that challenge their preconceived conclusions. They subject every piece of information to the touchstone of what is consistent with their "teachings." All inquiry and examination must and will be edited to accommodate to those "beliefs" even if the material has to be suppressed. This is the mind set of adolescence and is the normal and natural sequence of growth within the species. Yet, the unwillingness to move beyond adolescence into maturity is a disturbing phenomenon that is witnessed every day in any retirement community. Some people just refuse to grow up.

# Chapter 12
# CHRISTIANITY'S PAGAN ANTECEDENTS

"The common law existed while the Anglo-Saxons were yet pagans,
at a time when they had never yet heard the name of Christ
pronounced or knew that such a character existed."
Thomas Jefferson, letter to Major John Cartwright, June 5, 1824

At this point it would be helpful to examine the relationship between Christianity to its pagan antecedents. What began as a cult of Judaism, the new faith had demonstrable ties to paganism. One has only to observe the two most significant celebrations of "Christianism" (Easter and Christmas) to see the connection of "Christianism" to its pagan past. By the end of the fourth century, the church had utterly repudiated every hint of any connection with its pagan past, although the Council of Nicaea set the dates of Easter and Christmas using the formula employed by the pagans to establish their winter and spring solstice celebrations. The similarities between Christianity and Mithraism are so obvious that they could be interchangeable. The central story of the Christos predates Jesus with details of a virgin birth, a sacrificial death and a salvation story. So close was the story of Mithras that the Church Fathers identified it as a work of the Devil deliberately intended to parody the story of Christ. The fact that the cult of Mithras existed long before the Christian Messiah was born did not faze these defenders of the faith. They simply claimed that the devil was a sly old fox who had gone backwards in time to plant a man who would discredit the 'obvious' originality of the story of the Christ.

I cannot make it any clearer than Tom Harper does in his book, *The Pagan Christ*:

> "Far from being an original contribution to the world of religious thought….. Christianity was turned in the early centuries into a literalist copy of a resplendent spiritual forerunner. I will clearly document that there is nothing the Jesus of the Gospels either said of did— from the Sermon on the Mount to the miracles, from his flights as an infant from Herod to the Resurrection itself—that cannot be shown to have originated thousands of years before, in Egyptian Mystery rites and other sacred liturgies such as the Egyptian Book of the Dead. Everything—from the star in the east to Jesus' walking on water, from the angel's pronouncement to the slaughter of the innocents by Herod, from the temptation in the wilderness to the changing water into wine—already existed in the Egyptian sources. Egypt and its peoples had knelt at the shrine of the Madonna and Christ Isis and Horus for many long centuries before any allegedly historical Mary lifted a supposedly historical Jesus in her arms. But for all those centuries before the translation of the Rosetta Stone in 1822, the ancient key to all this Egyptian material had been lost. Centuries of blissful ignorance went by. Now, since the translation of the books of Old Egypt—the Egyptian Book of the Dead, the Pyramid Texts, the Amduat, and the Book of Thoth, for example—there is irrefutable proof that not one single doctrine, rite, tenet, or usage in Christianity was in reality a fresh contribution to the world of religion."[124]

Most Christians are aware that Jesus was not born on December 25th. Historians and scholars have known for a long time that this date was chosen because of the birth date of another famous individual called Mithras. The religion of Mithras preceded Christianity by roughly six hundred years and Mithraic worship covered a large portion of the ancient world from Iran to India. Mithraism was the prime competition to Christianity in the second through the fourth century, C.E. It is not surprising to learn that Mithras' birth was signaled by a shining star in the night sky and that he was born to a virgin in a cave, surrounded by shepherds who brought him gifts. Before he died, Mithras had a 'Last Supper' and later came back from the dead. He was said not to have died, but to have ascended to heaven from where he would return in the last days to raise the dead and judge them, sending the good to Paradise and the evil to Hell. He guaranteed his followers immortality after baptism. The followers of Mithras celebrated the atoning death of a savior who had risen on a Sunday. They celebrated a ceremony corresponding to the Catholic Mass during which they consumed consecrated bread and wine in memory of the last supper of Mithras—and during the ceremony they used hymns, bells, candles, and holy water. Indeed, they shared with Christians a long series of other beliefs and ritual practices, to the point that they were practically indistinguishable from each other in the eyes of the pagans and also of many Christians.

Another ancient pagan practice centered around the worship of Horus, one of the most significant deities of the ancient Egyptian religion. Here is a list showing the comparison between the ministry of Jesus and Horus:

- Jesus was baptized in the Jordan River. Horus was baptized in the River Eridanus by Anup, who was also beheaded.
- Both Jesus and Horus received their baptism at thirty.
- Jesus and Horus experience a temptation; Jesus had his Satan and Horus had his Sut.

- Both are performers of miracles. Horus was the prototype of Bacchus (the Greek counterpart is Dionysus).
- Both Jesus and Horus associate their teachings with stories about fishing, fishermen and nets. In the Egyptian Ritual, the four fishers pulled the dragnet through the waters to capture Horus.
- Jesus, in one gospel is asleep and was awakened by his disciples in a storm, where he then walked on water. In the Egyptian material, Horus emerges from the rage of a nocturnal storm and calms the waters.
- The Gospels follow the Egyptian emphasis upon the number three, showing that Jesus rose on the third day, while Horus rose in a new body of light on the third day.
- Jesus was the good shepherd, while Horus was seen as the Good Shepherd centuries before.
- Jesus said that he was the bread of life. Gerald Massey says that Horus also gave his flesh for food and his blood for drink.
- Jesus preached about being born twice. This concept is found in the Egyptian texts as well as in Hinduism.
- Horus rises up in glory and lifts all other people with him; this is reminiscent of Jesus' words about being 'lifted up' and drawing all men unto him.

If you ever have been to Egypt, as I have, you were struck with the similarity between the Egyptian ankh and the crucifix. The cross was a symbol in ancient religion long before it became the central icon of "Christianism." Wikipedia defines the ankh as the key of life, the key of the Nile, which the ancient Egyptian hieroglyphics character read as "eternal life." Egyptian gods are often portrayed carrying it by its loop, or bearing one in each hand, arms crossed over their chest. The ankh appears frequently in Egyptian tomb paintings and other art, often at the fingertips of a god or goddess in images that represent the deities of the afterlife conferring the gift of life on the dead person's mummy; this is thought to symbolize the act of conception. Additionally, an ankh was often carried by Egyptians as an amulet much like Christians wear the cross around their neck. This is another evidence of the influence of Ancient Egypt on the rites, symbols and rituals of "Christianism". No wonder the religious elite, in its effort to cover up its lie about our religious past, continued to try eliminating all traces of our pagan past through distortion, deceit, denial and demagoguery. Not content with the specious allegation that Satan had been behind the amazing resemblances between "Christianism" and paganism, the leaders of the church made every attempt to destroy the documents that would challenge their blatant dishonesty. Entire works on Mithraism were obliterated. In 379-395 C.E. Emperor Theodosius I made heresy illegal, thus effectively destroying Paganism. Church fathers, including Justin Martyr and Tertullian, attacked Mithraism claiming that they imitated central Christian rites and ceremonies. The fact is, I have been too kind in my assessment of this deliberate cover-up; they did everything in their power, through forgery and other fraud, book burning, character assassination, and murder itself for the purpose of destroying the crucial evidence of what had happened. In the least, this is certainly not a very good imitation of the life and message of Jesus Christ, whom they purport to emulate.

Alvin Boyd Kuhn, in his book, *Who is this King of Glory?*, says that the entire Christian Bible and its stories are now proven to have been transmitted from ancient Egypt's scrolls and papyri into the hands of later generations who didn't know their true origin or their fathomless meanings. Kuhn argues that: "Long after Egypt's voice, expressed through the inscribed hieroglyphics, was hushed in silence, the perpetuated relics of Egyptian wisdom, with their cryptic message utterly lost, were brought to the world by parties or ignorant zealots as a new body of truth. Only by fully acknowledging and regaining its parenthood in that sublime Pagan source will Christianity rise at last to its intended true nobility and splendor."[125]

Shall we brand this cover-up a conspiracy? I will leave that for the reader to decide. Another evidence of the distinction between Christianity and "Christianism" is the fact that a whole list of books that stood favorably in the eyes of the early Christian community at the start and for some time thereafter, were condemned and repudiated within less than two centuries. The Nag Hammadi Library contains many of these condemned books. They throw a radically different light on early Christianity and the interpretation of the teachings of Jesus. The Nag Hammadi Library is a collection of thirteen ancient codices containing over fifty texts. They were discovered in Upper Egypt in 1945. This immensely important discovery includes a large number of primary "Gnostic Gospels." These were texts once thought to have been entirely destroyed during the early Christian struggle to define "orthodoxy" (scriptures such as the Gospel of Thomas, the Gospel of Philip, and the Gospel of Truth). In the first century of the Christian era the term "Gnostic" came to denote a heterodox segment of the diverse new Christian community. Among early followers of Jesus, it appears there were groups who delineated themselves from the greater household of the Church by claiming not simply a belief in Christ and his message, but a "special witness" or revelatory experience of the divine. It was this experience or gnosis that set the true followers of Christ apart, or so they asserted. Stephan Hoeller explains that these Christians held a conviction that direct, personal and absolute knowledge of the authentic truths of existence is accessible to human beings; and, moreover, that the attainment of such knowledge must always constitute the supreme achievement of human life.[126] I am not arguing for a return to Gnosticism, since this philosophy has many aspects which contradict

Jesus' teachings about God and himself. What I advocate is a return to the mysticism that was a part of the Gnostic teaching.

———⋅—⋅———

# Chapter 13
# OUR HERITAGE ROOTED IN ANTIQUITY

The Christian religion, when divested of the rags in which they [the clergy] have enveloped it, and brought to the original purity and simplicity of its benevolent institutor (Jesus), is a religion of all others most friendly to
liberty, science, and the freest expansion of the human mind.
—Thomas Jefferson, to Moses Robinson, 1801.

Most American Christians seem to believe that Christianity was born in a vacuum, totally ignoring the history of other religions, which date back to the Sumerians. Comparative hierologists have discovered records of over thirty Savior-God religions, many of whom had some form of a virgin birth, a crucifixion, and a resurrection story.

Was this a copy-cat situation or a perennial expression of some Universal Pattern? The various Savior-Gods had the following similar traits:

- They were born on or near Christmas
- Their mothers were virgins.
- They were born in a cave or stable.
- They worked for the salvation of humanity.
- They were called Saviors, mediators, healers, etc.
- They were overcome by evil powers.
- A descent into Hell was made by them.
- after being slain, they arose and ascended to heaven.
- They were commemorated by Eucharistic rites.
- Many of these Savior-Gods were believed to return.

The "Founder of Christian Theology," Augustine, seemed to know this fact. Here is his quote: **"That which is known as the Christian religion existed among the ancients, and never did not exist; from the very beginning of the human race until the time when Christ came in the flesh, at which time the true religion, which already existed, began to be called Christianity"**[127] This astonishing declaration was made in the early fourth century of our era. Had this quote been common knowledge among the Christian populous, the power of ecclesiastical clerics would have been greatly diminished and the rise of fundamental Christianity curtailed. This quote challenges the belief that Christianity was a completely new and the first true religion in world history. The following very long passage is included because of its profound implications.

Alvin Boyd Kuhn provides this commentary on the quotation by Augustine:

"This astonishing declaration was made in the early fourth century of our era. It can be asserted with little chance of refutation that if this affirmation of the pious Augustine had not sunk out of sight, but had been kept in open view through the period of Western history, the whole course of that history would have been vastly altered for the better. It is only too likely the case that the obvious implications of the passage were of such a nature that its open exploitation was designedly frowned upon by the ecclesiastical authorities in every age. It held the kernel of a great truth the common knowledge of which would have been a stumbling block in the way of the perpetuation of priestly power over the general Christian mind. It would have provoked inquiry and disarmed the ecclesiastical prestige of much of its power."[128]

The commentary further states:

"For what is it that the Christian saint actually says: "It stands as hardly less than a point-blank repudiation of all the chief asseverations on which the structure of Christian tradition rests. Every child born to Christian parents in eighteen centuries has been indoctrinated with the unqualified belief that Christianity was completely new, and the first true, religion in world history, that it was vouchsafed to the world by God himself and brought to earth by the sole divine emissary ever commissioned to convey God's truth to mankind; that it flashed out amid the lingering murks of Pagan darkness as the first ray of true light to illumine the path way of evolution for the safe treading of human feet. All previous religion was the superstitious product of primitive childishness of mind. Christianity was the first piercing of the long night of black heathenism by the benignant gift of God. Augustine shatters this illusion and this jealously preserved phantom of blind credulity. 'From remotest antiquity', he asserts, 'there has always existed in the world the true religion.'"[129]

Augustine was not the only church father who asserted this astounding revelation. Eusebius, the early church historian, penned a lengthy statement asserting that while the name Christ is new, the principles of the faith are by no means new. This idea was echoed in the work of Justin Martyr, a chapter entitled, "Against Celsius." In the debate we find Celsius saying, "The Christian religion contains nothing but what Christians hold in common with the heathen, nothing new." In defense, Justin Martyr was reduced to blaming this observation on the devil in these words: "In having reached the devil's ears that the prophets had foretold that Christ would come…he (the devil) set the heathen poets to bring forward a great many who should be called son of Jove (that is sons of God); the devil laying his scheme in this to get men to imagine that the true history of Christ was of the same character as the prodigious fables and poetic stories."[130]

If this argument were not so serious, it would be laughable. It is reminiscent of Flip Wilson's line, "The Devil made me do it." Harpur points out that numerous church fathers blamed the devil on this "planted deception," including Tertullian (ca.160-220 C.E.), bishop of North Africa, who again blamed the devil by saying that the devil imitates even the main part of the Divine (Christian) mysteries. "He baptizes his worshipers in water and makes them believe that purifies them from their crimes!...Mithras sets his mark on the forehead of his soldiers; he celebrates the offering of bread; he offers an image of the resurrection...He limits his chief priests to a single marriage; he even has his virgins and ascetics." Harpur comments on this attempt to blot out all links between the Christian body of doctrine and any pagan material. "The top Church authorities were not content with the original, specious allegation that Satan had been behind all the amazing resemblances—they even talked of 'anticipated plagiarism,' charging that the devil stole the rites, doctrines, and dogmas centuries before they became accepted by the Church—so they destroyed as far as possible the entire pagan record to obliterate the evidence of their own dishonesty."[131] The church needs to have an honest assessment of its failure to embrace its pagan ancestors by admitting to the truth about its past.

Is a cover-up equivalent to a lie? I was one of those children who were indoctrinated with this pious lie about our religious past. Mind you, my parents and theirs were also the victims of this extensive cover-up and false information by the religious elite. Most Christians are totally oblivious to the relationship between Christianity and antecedent religious influences, most particularly those stemming from ancient Egypt. I think that it is quite possible that the religious elite did not want the populous to know the truth about the fact that true religion has always existed. It went under a variety of designations: Hermeticism in ancient Egypt, Orphism in Greece; Zoroastrianism in Persia; Brahamanism in

India; Taoism in China; Shintoism in Japan and China. It was dramatized and ritualized by the Mystery Cults, no matter how primitive or perverted its expression. There are some who think that the Mass is a fairly primitive and cultish practice; so we need to be careful not to make judgments on these expressions of ancient religious practices. Basic to those ancient religions is the concept of the Christos, the Divine principle in every person. Possibly Paul unintentionally stumbled on this understanding when he wrote: "Christ in you, your hope of glory,"[132] although he had a much more limited understanding of the word, Christ.

The concept of the "Indwelling Christ" is heart and center to the thesis of this book. This idea has been called "The Third Jesus" by Deepak Chopra in his book by that title. Charles Fillmore made a distinction between the Jesus of history, the manifestation of that Universal Presence in the man Jesus and the Christ of faith. Khun seems to pull no punches in his condemnation of historical Christianity in what he calls their failure to connect the ancient idea of the Egyptian Christos and the manifestation of that presence in the personality of Jesus. I insert a long quote from Kuhn because it calls for a challenge for the proponents of "Christianism" to respond to his charge with equal scholarship and clarity:

> "Egypt had known a Jesus who long antedated the Gospel Messiah and who presents to the student some one hundred and eighty items of identity, similarity, and correspondence in word, deed and function with his later copy. But Egypt's Christ was not a living person. It would have been equally fatal to Christianity if he had been. But the fact of his non-historicity rises now out of the past that Christianity thought it had sealed in oblivion forever, to strike the death-knell of a false and spurious religion. The Gospels' 'life' of Jesus turns out to be nothing but the garbled and fragmentary copy of an Egyptian prototype who never lived, but was a

purely typal dramatic figure, portraying the divinity in man. With this one revelation of lost truth the structure of historical Christianity toppled to the ground. It must be replaced by a purely spiritual Christianity"[133]

In 1945 the Nag Hammadi Library was unearthed and its revelations jolted the theological world. Basic to its teachings is an insight into the esoteric side of Jesus' message. In these instructions we find passages such as: "Abandon the search for God and the creation and other matter of similar sort. Look for him by taking yourself as the starting point. Learn who it is within you. To know the self is to know God." Elaine Pagels[134] points out that there are three essential strands to the esoteric message of Christ, as revealed in the Gnostic gospels: (1) Self-knowledge is knowledge of God; the highest self and the divine are identical. (2) The living Jesus of these texts speaks of illusion and enlightenment, not of sin and repentance (3) Jesus is presented not as Lord but as spiritual guide.

There are those who believe that we can understand Jesus' teachings if we can identify the historical Jesus and identify his actual words. An attempt to make this discovery was boldly taken by the Jesus Seminar.[135] The Jesus Seminar is a group of 250 scholars who are making the same mistake that Schweitzer made in his search for the historical Jesus. It is a laudable quest but one doomed to failure since we do not have enough "original" material to assist us in this quest. In the following comments I will give a brief overview of this group and their mission.

The definitive work on the Jesus Seminar was edited by Robert Funk and Roy W. Hoover in a book entitled *The Five Gospels*. The Jesus Seminar believes that they can ascertain and identify the historical Jesus by dissecting the first four gospels. The publication of *The Quest for the Historical Jesus*, by Albert Schweitzer, effectively put a stop for decades to the work on the Historical Jesus as a sub-discipline of New Testament studies, until the study was resurrected by the Jesus Seminar. This group completely ignored the words of Albert Schweitzer, who at the end of his book, said: "The Jesus of Nazareth who came forward publicly as the Messiah, who preached the ethic of the Kingdom of God, who founded the Kingdom of Heaven upon earth, and died to give His work its final consecration, never had any existence. He is a figure designed by rationalism, endowed with life by liberalism, and clothed by modern theology in an historical garb. He comes to us as One unknown, without a name, as of old, by the lake-side; He came to those men who knew Him not. He speaks to us the same words 'Follow thou me!' and sets us to the tasks which He has to fulfill for our time. He commands. And to those who obey Him, whether they be wise or simple, He will reveal Himself in the toils, the conflicts, the sufferings which they shall pass through in His fellowship, and, as an ineffable mystery, they shall learn in their own experience Who He Is."[10]

# Chapter 14
# THE CONTRIBUTION OF HERETICS

"And the day will come, when the mystical generation of Jesus,
by the Supreme Being as His Father, in the womb of a virgin,
will be classed with the fable of the generation of Minerva,
in the brain of Jupiter." Thomas Jefferson

The word "heretic" is one of the most misused words in the Christian Community. The colloquial usage implies anyone who does not agree with orthodoxy. It is usually used derogatorily. Historically, it has been used as an accusation levied against members of another group who had beliefs which conflicted with those of the accusers. Basically, heresy is an opinion held in opposition to that of authority or orthodoxy. The proper meaning of heretic, etymologically, is "one who chooses." In other words, heresy is the freedom to disagree and to embrace another pathway in contradistinction to orthodoxy. Again, the method of determining who was right was democracy. The vote determined the authenticity and truth of the movement, not whether it was true to the teachings of the supposed founder of the faith. In past history, the Roman Catholic Church executed anyone who had a different opinion from church dogma. I prefer to define heresy in a more positive light. "To think" implies that you will have different opinions from others on almost every subject including religion. The church's cruel treatment of heretics has been a dark stain on the history of "Christianism."

Many of Christianity's early and most learned Church Fathers were later excommunicated from The Church and declared to be heretics. Three hundred years after his death, the established church declared Origen, a pupil of St. Clement of Alexandria, to be a heretic worthy of death. The church has been known to dig up the bones of Christians and burn them, just because they deviated from "official doctrine." Origen was an enlightened scholar, who taught reincarnation, karma, and universal salvation. He was opposed to a literalistic approach to Scripture and to the reduction of the profundities of spiritual truth to the vulgarities of simplistic outer religion (exotericism). Origen once stated that a literal understanding of "Christ crucified" was a doctrine only fit for children in the faith.

Gnosticism is another early Christian teaching that fell into disrepute, as the church came under the control of the religious elite. That Gnosticism was in the mainstream of Christianity is witnessed by the history of one of its most influential teachers, Valentinus. He may have been in consideration during the mid-second century for election as the Bishop of Rome. Born in Alexandria around 100 C.E., Valentinus distinguished himself at an early age as an extraordinary teacher and leader in the highly educated and diverse Alexandrian Christian community. In mid-life he migrated from Alexandria to the Church's evolving capital, Rome, where he played an active role in the public affairs of the Church. A prime characteristic of Gnosticism was its claim to be keepers of sacred traditions, gospels, rituals, and successions. These were esoteric matters for which many Christians were either not properly prepared or simply not inclined to consider. Valentinus, true to this Gnostic predilection, apparently professed to have received a special apostolic sanction through Theudas, a disciple and initiate of the Apostle Paul. Though an influential member of the Roman church in the mid-second century, by the end of his life Valentinus had been forced from the public eye and branded a heretic by the developing Orthodox Church.

Valentinus was not the only casualty of this growing orthodoxy. By the end of the fourth century, many of the early church's pioneers and leaders had been pronounced heretics from the true faith by the developing religious elite.

Another distinction between Christianity and "Christianism" is the use of the mystical, allegorical mode of interpreting the sacred Scriptures. The parables of Jesus are an illustration of the metaphorical use of stories which were not intended to be interpreted literally. By the fourth century, this tradition had been supplanted by the literal-historical approach to the Scriptures. Out of this redaction came the emphasis on trying to discover the historical Jesus by seeking to appeal to the words written about him in the New Testament.

Let us examine one of the seven signs used by the Apostle John in his gospel to prove that Jesus is the only Son of God. It is the story of the raising of Lazarus. One significant thing about this story disturbed me long before I learned of its Egyptian antecedents. Providing this was a literal event, it would have commanded attention of the populous extending far beyond Bethany and would have been the seminal event in the life of Jesus. Historians, such as Josephus, would have recorded the event giving it bold coverage in his history of the Jews. The secular witnesses were noticeably silent. Even if Josephus had not heard of this stupendous event, the writers of the first three gospels certainly knew about it. Why is it that they chose to ignore the most important event in the contemporary life of Jesus? The story appears solely in the Fourth Gospel. Could it be that they never heard about it because it never happened as literal fact? John believed that it was so important that it was the immediate cause of the crucifixion. This interpretation is contradicted by the writers of the Synoptic Gospels, who plainly place the cleansing of the temple as the trigger for the consequences of holy week. This is important information because the cleansing of the temple comes right at the beginning of Jesus' public ministry, according to John. It is placed at the end of his ministry by Matthew, Mark and Luke.

If you are as puzzled as I was, maybe the answer lies in the ancient past within the tombs of Egypt. One has only to read the writings of Kuhn and study the research of Gerald Massey and other Egyptian scholars to clear up this cryptic account. Read as pure historical fact, this story is plagiarism of the boldest kind. The story of this myth's allegorical antecedent is the raising of El-Asar by Horus. Unless we wish to blame Satan for a trick of history, we must take seriously this information presented by Tom Harpur. He summarizes this comparison as follows:

"In the Egyptian Book of the Dead, Anu, called Heliopolis in Greek (meaning 'city of the sun') was they theological name of an actual Egyptian city where the rites of the death, burial, and resurrection of Osiris or Horus were enacted each year.... Anu was precisely a place where units of divine consciousness (or souls) go in their symbolic 'death' in every human incarnation and later rise again to glory. Anu was called, among other things, the place of 'multiplying bread.'.... The Hebrews added their prefix for 'house,' beth, to Anu and produced Beth-Anu, or the House of Anu..... The point here is that when we read the Egyptian text, we find that the Egyptian Christ, Horus, performed a great miracle at Anu, or Bethany. He raised his father, Osiris, from the dead, calling him in the cave to 'rise and come forth.'.... When the Hebrews took up the name of Osiris, or Lord Osiris, they used the Hebrew word for 'Lord,' el—hence El-Asar. Later on, the Romans, speaking Latin, of course, took El-Asar and added the us ending used for most male names. The result was El-Asar-us. In time, the initial e 'wore off,' as linguists describe it, and the s in Asar changed to z, its constant companion in language. Thus, we have Lazarus, the Osiris of the Beth-Anu story. One final detail: in the Johannine account, Jesus makes the surprising assertion that Lazarus is not dead but only sleeping. The same thing was said many centuries earlier, in the ancient scripts of Osiris in Egypt: 'That is Osiris who is not dead but sleeping in Anu the place of his repose, awaiting the call that bids him come forth today.' In the text of the Har-Hetep, the speaker, who personates Horus in the drama, is he who comes to awaken Asar (Osiris) out of his sleep."[136]

Harpur goes on to reconcile the two, regarding intention. "The Egyptian Ritual was certainly mythical in character—that is, it was intended to celebrate the eventual resurrection to radiant glory of the individual's true self, the inner Christ. Similarly, the author/editor of John had no intent to deceive the reader with 'false history.' The purpose, rather, was exactly the same—to convey, in the vivid context of a fictional story, the esoteric, spiritual truth of our own final victory over the grave itself, our resurrection"[137]

Let me summarize what I have said by encapsulating it in the following list:

- Christianity began as a cult with ties to pagan origins.
- Books that were highly regarded at the start of the movement and for some time thereafter were condemned and violently repudiated within less than two centuries.
- Several doctrines that were held in great esteem in the initial period, such as universal salvation, were later refuted.
- The fourth century has been pronounced as heretical.
- The mystical/allegorical method of interpreting the sacred Scripture was replaced by a wholly literal/historical approach.

In the late 1300s John Wycliffe translated the scriptures from the Latin. About 44 years after his death, the Catholic Inquisition dug up his bones and burned them calling him an arch-heretic. In the 1500's William Tyndale sought to translate the Bible into the language of the common people, English. He could not gain approval from the Catholic institution, so he worked as an outlaw on the run in Europe, translating the Bible. He was eventually captured, condemned and executed in 1536. It is because of people like these men, Tyndale and Wycliffe, that we have the scriptures today. Heretics have made a major contribution in the quest for truth and the preservation of freedom, which is imperative if one is to find truth.

# Chapter 15
# WORDS HAVE NO MEANING

---

"In matters of style, swim with the current;
In matters of principle, stand like a rock."
Thomas Jefferson

Words have no meaning; they only have usages. A social revolutionist once said, "Change the meaning (usage) of words and you can change and control a culture." What he said is certainly true regarding key New Testament words that have been mistranslated. The word "religion" has been changed as have many words that are used to define religious dogma and doctrine. The word, religion comes from the Latin, *religio*, which means "that which binds together." You can see how much the original meaning has changed, since contemporary religion tends to divide people more often than it unites.

Almost all New Testament words used to define dogma have been drastically changed. The word "sin" (*hamartia* in Greek) is an example of this change. The word in its original usage is an archery term. It means to miss the mark. No archer would ever do penitence over missing the target. Rather, he would choose another arrow and shoot again, thus using the sin as a feedback device to insure his aim. The prodigal son did not "sin" against his father. Listen to his mantra, "Father I have sinned and done this evil in thy sight." The father in this story did not even hear these words, but fell on his neck and kissed him and called for the fatted calf to be prepared in celebration. His words are also revealing. "This, my son, who was dead is now alive." In this parable, Jesus implies that we do not sin against God; we sin against ourselves. There are always consequences to our behavior. The prodigal son suffered the karma of his choices, but when he "came to himself" (awakened) he experienced the grace of unconditional love. The awakening process implies that he was asleep and merely woke up. It does not imply a radical transformation generated by a belief in some sacrificial interpretation of Jesus' crucifixion. This is Paul's gospel, not Jesus'.

Orthodox Christianity has adopted a concept of original sin that seems to be original in the world of "Christianism." Original sin refers to the origin or motive behind everything that we always do. In other words, we are not sinners because we occasionally sin; we "sin occasionally" because we are always sinners. The doctrine of original sin comes from two Old Testament sources; one from the story of Adam's expulsion from the Garden of Eden and the second from the story of David's depression over his adultery with Bathsheba.

From the Catholic online encyclopedia we have this official definition of sin: "Original sin may be taken to mean: (1) the sin that Adam committed; or (2) a consequence of this first sin, the hereditary stain with which we are born on account of our origin or descent from Adam.

From the earliest times the latter sense of the word "sin" was more common, as may be seen by St. Augustine's statement: "The deliberate sin of the first man is the cause of original sin."[138] It is the hereditary stain that is dealt with here. As to the sin of Adam, we have not to examine the circumstances in which it was committed nor make the exegesis of the third chapter of Genesis.[139] I suppose the rationale here is, "Believe it because I said so." Certainly this text needs examination and exegesis (scholarly examination of the text). The doctrine is not found in Judaism, and its scriptural foundation is found only one place in the New Testament, the teachings of Paul the Apostle (Romans 5:13-21 and I Corinthians 15:22). Orthodoxy prefers using the term "ancestral sin" which indicates that original sin is hereditary. It did not remain only Adam and Eve's. As life passes from them to all of their descendants, so does original sin.

We must ponder the observation of an American atheist who said, "Christianity is—must be!—totally committed to the special creation as described in Genesis, and Christianity must fight with its full might against the theory of evolution. And here is why. In Romans 5:12, we read that 'sin entered the world through one man, and through sin—death, and thus death has spread through the whole human race because everyone has sinned.' The whole justification of Jesus' life and death is predicated on the existence of Adam and the forbidden fruit he and Eve ate. Without the original sin, who needs to be redeemed? Without Adam's fall into a life of constant sin terminated by death, what purpose is there to Christianity? None!" [141]

The problem here is that the author does not make a distinction between primitive Christianity (which focuses on the teachings of Jesus) and the institution that followed (of which Paul was the founder), which focused on his sacrificial death. It is an interpretation of Jesus' life and death that ties these events to a soteriological (salvation) conclusion. Gustaf Aulen has argued that there are more logical reasons why Jesus lived and died, the major one being the willingness to give his life for that in which he believed. Aulen connects the resurrection with victory over death, which has no saving value other than a demonstration of what all men will one day experience.

Most liberal scholars see the material in Genesis as mythological and not literal history. Jesus was not concerned with Adam and his Original Sin. From the book of Genesis all of the way through the ending of the Old Testament, there isn't the slightest hint of Original Sin as being inherited by all humans through Adam. Even more importantly, where is there any indication that this sin must be "redeemed" eventually by Jesus? By all appearances, Paul's interpretation is not really warranted by the actual story found in the third chapter of Genesis.

The second reference comes from Psalm 51, the repentant prayer of David that left him in a moment of pain and despair. David concludes that he must have been born in sin or else how could he have done such a dastardly deed. Paul takes this passage, born out of remorse and despair, and gives it a central place in his theology. When you compare this Psalm to another of David's writings, when he was in a high state of consciousness, you have a different picture of man. In Psalm 8 we find a wonderful tribute to the Divinity of Man. He says:

"When I consider the heavens, the work of thy fingers, the moon and stars, which thou hast ordained, what is man that thou are mindful of him? And the son of man, that thou visitest him? For thou has made him but a little lower than God, and crownest him with glory and honor. Thou makest him to have dominion over the works of thy hands; thou hast put all things under his feet."[142]

Yet another picture of man from the book of Genesis reveals a glowing picture, not a sinful one. "God created man is His own image, in the image of God created He man, male and female created He them."[143] We have a choice to choose between the two pictures of man's conditions presented in the Bible. We can choose to see man as a sinner or we can choose to see him as a child of God made in His image, waiting for an unlimited potential to be released and channeled for undreamed of deeds, for unimagined good.

The comic strip *Peanuts* is a great example of the ubiquitous influence of the concept of original sin that permeates our society. Shultz presents the yearly saga of Lucy badgering Charlie Brown to trust her one more time to hold the football for his place-kicking adventure. Shultz presents a rather pessimistic view of human nature in this running gag that always ends the same with Lucy pulling the ball away and Charlie falling flat on his back. Listen to the dialogue: Lucy: "Why don't you let me hold the ball for you Charlie Brown?" Charlie: "Do you think I'm crazy? Do you think you can fool me with the same trick every year?" Lucy: "Oh, I won't pull the ball away, Charlie Brown, I promise you. I give you my bonded word." Charlie: "All right, I'll trust you; I have an undying faith in human nature! I believe that people who want to change can do so, and I believe that they should be given a chance to prove themselves. "AAugh! Whmp!" You can hear the thud. Charles Schultz uses humor to depreciate the good that is characteristic of Charlie Brown.

There have been voices down through the centuries who have protested this grotesque doctrine of original sin, but they have been condemned as heretics. Pelagius was such a voice. He was condemned as a heretic at the third Council of Ephesus in 431 C.E. They said of him that he was, "Accustomed to call attention to the capacity and character of human nature and to show what it was able to accomplish." For this lofty view of man, the church burned people at the stake.

Jonathan Livingston Seagull spoke of very simple things such as it is right for a gull to fly, that freedom is the very nature of his being, that whatever stands against that freedom must be set aside, be it ritual or superstition or limitation in any form. "Why is it," Jonathan puzzled, "That the hardest thing in the world is to convince a bird that he is free, that he can prove it for himself if he'd just spend a little time practicing? Why should that be so hard?"

Another New Testament word that has been totally corrupted by mistranslation (either by incompetence or by deliberate effort) is the word, "repent." The Greek word for repentance is *Metanoia*, which means change of mind. The

Greek particle *meta* is found in several words of comparatively ordinary usage, such as metaphor, metaphysics and
metamorphosis. The word metaphor means transference
of meaning which is to speak beyond the literal meaning
of the word. Metaphysics is the study of that which is beyond purely observable physical science. Metamorphosis is
the term used to describe the transformation in form from
a grub to a butterfly. The particle *meta*, therefore, means
transference, or transformation, or beyond-ness. The other
part of the word translated repentance *noia* is from the
Greek word, nous, which means mind. The word, *metanoia*
has to do with the transformation of the mind, which is its
essential meaning.

The English word "repentance" is derived from the Latin *poenitare* which means to feel sorry or regret. The word
*metanoia* implies a new mind, not new emotions. It is a
mental change, not a moral change, which is based on
being sorry for a wrong that is done. A new mind brings
with it a new approach to everything in life; it has nothing
to do with penance. When Paul uses the word "repent" in
II Corth. 7:8-9, he uses a Greek word which is equivalent to
the Latin *poenitet* which is what the English word repentance actually means. Why do the English translators insist
on translating two different Greek words, with totally different meanings by using the same word, repentance? It is either by incompetence or by design. To change from within
gives power to the person, who makes the change. To be
controlled from without by the religious elite, by doing penance, gives power to those dispensing the requirements of
the penance, thus giving the elite the power of absolution.
The mistranslation of these two Greek words, *harmartia*
and *metanoia* is a blatant example of the big religious lie,
that the religious elite tells for the purpose of controlling the
masses. The word "radical" is another word that has been
misused or misunderstood. It originally referred to the juice
in fruits and vegetables, the moisture provided through the

roots (radix in Latin). It later came to mean the essence or substance of things. Radical does not mean "far out," but rather "far in." Do you realize now radically Jesus cut across the collective consciousness of the people of his age? His behavior and words were shocking to the exclusive Jewish orientation of his day. The story of the Good Samaritan illustrates this radicalism in the behavior of Jesus. What makes this story so important is the selection of the Samaritan as the main character in the story. It is a fact of history that the Judean Jews had no dealings with the Samaritans and considered them to be of lower quality racially and religiously. The city of Samaria, from which the province took its name, was the capital of the old kingdom of Israel that had been conquered by Sargon II of Assyria in 722 B.C. Sargon deported thousands of the Hebrew inhabitants and imported various foreign tribes. During the passage of years, the Hebrews who had been left in Israel intermarried with the foreigners, thus producing a mixed race, a mixture of Assyrian and Hebrew. The religion of the Samaritans was similar to that of the Jews; however, the Samaritans rejected the writings of the great Hebrew Prophets as valid scripture. A Judean Jew felt himself vastly superior to a Samaritan and would not pass through the latter's territory if he could avoid it.

In this story, Jesus portrays for us the three great ideologies or philosophies that predominate in this world. This is a perfect picture of the motives and the forces that dominate the actions of man. The three ideas can be expressed in a sentence of five words. We only need to change the position of the words. Here they are. What is thine is mine, I'll take it. What is mine is mine, I'll keep it. What is mine is thine, I'll share it.

# Chapter 16
# IDEAS HAVE CONSEQUENCES

"What is it that men cannot be made to believe!"
Thomas Jefferson to Richard Henry Lee, April 22, 1786.

The Christmas story is just that, a story. On the surface, the story is innocuous and very compelling, because it tells about the birth of a baby in a stable, shepherds attending his birth, wise men bringing gifts, and an unusual edict of a jealous king. Since ideas have unintended consequences, the birth narratives have unwittingly contributed to the anti-sexual bias of the organized church. The emphasis by Matthew and Luke on the virgin birth has created a culture within the church that preaches abstinence over healthy sexual engagement. It is to be noted that the other three writers of the New Testament (Mark, John and Paul) did not mention Jesus' birth much less emphasize the virginal aspect of his birth. Paul did mention the fact that "Jesus was born of woman."[144]

The Christmas story found in Matthew and Luke is a story where only Hallmark Cards can harmonize the conflicting accounts of Jesus' presence in Egypt and the temple at Jerusalem at the same time. Chronologically, it is impossible. Since Herod of Matthew's account was in rule when Jesus was born (B.C. 4-6) and Luke has Jesus born when Cyrenius was governor of Syria (C.E. 6), one writer said that the birth of Jesus was a miracle of a ten-year pregnancy. We cannot escape the evidence that, at least on one level, the Christmas story is about sexuality. Granted, this story is about anti-sex, placing abstinence as a preferable practice for women. Sexuality has always been a dilemma for many religious people. Their religion often inhibits and controls sexual behavior, but the adherents often practice something totally different than their lofty and ungrounded beliefs. Recent media has been filled with stories of preachers who rant against homosexuality and in private actually practice the very thing that they condemn. Priests have been prosecuted for pedophilia, bringing open shame to the church. The Jews have historically been in an emotional dichotomy about sexuality and the role of women in their religion. Some of the great religious leaders in Jewish antiquity were women, notably Queen Esther and Ruth. They were lauded as paragons of religious zeal. "Christianism" has, from its inception, diminished the role of women within the church, especially in the arena of leadership. The Christmas story has helped set the stage for this suppression.

Since the Christmas story has a strong sexual overtone, one is inclined to ask, "What's so great about virginity?" Virginity is age appropriate. Children have no business having sex, because they are not old enough or mature enough to handle the intense emotional and psychology responsibility that comes with premature sexual activity. This may very well cause serious psychological problems later in life, if not warp their sense of mature sexuality. The emphasis found in Matthew and Luke on Jesus' virgin birth is found deficient after careful scholarly examination. Matthew takes his word "virgin" from a Greek translation (Septuagint) of Isaiah's text found in Isaiah 7:14. This passage is used as a proof text for the doctrine of the virgin birth. Every major scholar that I researched agrees that the passage in Isaiah does not refer to a woman without sexual intercourse prior to conception (which is the correct meaning of the phrase, virgin birth). Even Matthew and Luke are not talking about a virgin birth; they are referring to a virgin conception.

Because the Christian church has been anti-sexual in its philosophical orientation, this attitude has relegated women, within the church, to three positions. They have been glorified as mothers and virgins (an impossible biological dichotomy to harmonize) or they have been classified as prostitutes. This has placed women in an untenable position, relegating them to the status of second- class citizens within the church. There are some churches which have featured classes on the topic of how women should be subservient to their husbands.

Let me use the Bible to prove my point about this unusual thesis. There are two genealogies in Matthew and Luke. Luke inserts the genealogy of Jesus after the birth story in the account of John the Baptist. In this genealogy there are only men listed, no women. But Matthew has a different genealogy, one that includes four women, all of whom were identified with some form of sexual impropriety. The KJV simply sprinkles the women among the male predominated list. However, the later more conservative translations recognized the dilemma that this list exposed and tried to minimize the obvious damaging implications. The revisionists stated it in this fashion: "Judah the father of Perez and Zerah, whose mother was Tamar. These four sexually-compromised women are Tamar, a victim of incest and rape;[146] Rehab, the harlot;[147] Ruth, the sexual aggressor;[148] and Bathsheba, the wife of Uriah.[149]. I find it puzzling that Matthew, a Jewish writer, would include women in his genealogical list, especially women with sexual misconduct as their predominate epitaph. Was this an attempt to deal with the rumors that no doubt swirled around Mary's predicament? Could Matthew have been "hedging his bet," suggesting that God could use women who were tainted with sexual sin to accomplish His Divine purpose? Even Joseph had serious reservations about this matter until he was confronted with the announcement in a dream that the conception was "of the Holy Spirit."

Dan Brown, in his book *The Da Vinci Code*, has done some of us a favor by restoring a conversation about the role of Mary Magdalene and Jesus, a role that has serious sexual implications. In my community there was a mass picketing of the movie due to the implication that Jesus had sex. This was more than the locals could tolerate, since sex was something in which even their parents would not engage. So distorted was my upbringing on this topic that my previous comment is obviously biographical. The conflict over sex is not just an issue limited to the Christian church. Other religions, especially the Muslim religion, are conflicted over this subject. The Sharia Law demanding the wearing of a burqa is evidence of the anti-sexual bias of the Muslim religion. They place all the responsibility for temptation on the women, instead of the men; this practice is also characteristic of Judaism.

In 591 C.E., Pope Gregory the Great delivered a Christmas message in which he labeled Mary Magdalene a prostitute. This is a completely ungrounded supposition on the part of that Pope who mistakenly identified Mary Magdalene as the unnamed sinner referred to in Luke 7. However, the Second Vatican Council removed the prostitute label in 1969 after much debate and Biblical evidence that there was more than one Mary and that Mary of Magdalene and the unnamed sinner were two different figures.

Perhaps no figure in church history is as controversial or mysterious as Mary Magdalene, a devout follower of Jesus. Mary followed him to the very end, and was the first to witness his resurrection. She has been labeled such things as a prostitute, Jesus' wife, apostle and writer of the *Gnostic Gospel of Mary*, and the mother of Jesus' child. Although her name has been cleared of the prostitution label, the mysterious life of Mary Magdalene is still heavily studied and strongly debated, especially in recent times. After Jesus' death, the controversy around Mary Magdalene's life began. Believed to be Jesus' favorite disciple by the apostles, Mary is asked to reveal secret teachings given to her by Jesus while consoling the apostles. After her revelation, she has a disagreement with Peter about Jesus' teachings. This is the beginning of strengthening of Peter's role in early Christianity and the lessening of Mary's role.

What is the practical application for such information that I have presented today? First, we must be able to distinguish between fact and myth. A fact is an event that always requires interpretation. A myth is a universal truth that transcends the literary vehicle that carries the truth. The focus is on the message, not the messenger. Second, we must have a healthy understanding and experience of sexuality. We must learn to celebrate and honor our humanity as a major part of who we are. We are both spiritual and material, and we get into trouble when we try to separate the two. Our engagement in sexual activity is not to be dictated by the Catholic Church which cannot solve its sexual issues within their own clergy. Third, we must insist that the church move into the 21st century and honor the role of women in the church by opening its doors to women ministers, women priests and women bishops. Fourth, we must speak our truth without fear of intimidation or contradiction by emotionally laden religious people who do not know the facts about what the Bible teaches regarding women. Women are not second-class citizens in the church and should not be treated that way.

The plunge of "Christianism" into ascetic (abstaining from sex) morbidity started with the apostle Paul who led the drive toward the crucifixion of the flesh on behalf of the salvation of the soul. The body of man is to his soul as the horse is to the rider. By no means is the horse to be beaten into helplessness, abused, injured, or crippled. He is to be maintained, indeed, at the fullest vigor of his body. The ascetic Christian attitude toward the body stands as one of the supreme afflictions and miscarriages of all times. The Pagans had a high regard for the human body, which led to the historical clash between Christianism and paganism. There is a need to return to the saner and loftier moralities of pagan wisdom. Instead of viewing the physical body as evil, the pagans rendered it as beautiful. Love of beauty became a deadly Christian sin. Many in "Christianism" regard the body as the devil's foul creation. The practice of asceticism is the most tragic error of "Christianism," in that it produced conditions so unnatural as to shipwreck the mind as well as the body. Matter is not essentially evil, and the body is not the source of sin. This philosophy demeans women and reduces them to second class citizens, for they become objects of that which is to be avoided by the leaders of the church. Women were regarded as the evil seducers of men. This is an absurdly contorted philosophy, which led one Christian monk to plunge into an icy pond to quench his burning desires.

The ethics of Jesus' kingdom is not an ethic of rules; it is an ethic of consciousness. On the subject of sex, the church has been influenced by the Gnosticism that it once denounced. The Gnostics saw the body as evil. Nothing that belongs to us must be denied conscious recognition and acceptance as a genuine part of our totality. Sexual urges are a part of the perfectly natural human condition. We cannot resist these urges with impunity. When Jesus refers to one's sexual imagination as equivalent to adultery, he is suggesting that in matters of sex, we need a higher law than that of ecclesiastical legislation. That higher law is consciousness. The ethic of the kingdom requires that all sides of human nature are to become conscious, but no one side is to predominate at the expense of the other. It is the balance that we seek in every aspect of our life.

This is the result of a horrid misconception of the doctrine of sin, which has become a mental torture for a whole body of Christians for ages. It has turned what might have been a life of joy into a nightmare of dread and delusion for those who are supposed to represent the teacher of Galilee who said: "I have come that you might have joy and have it more abundantly."[149]

Why should we even bother to celebrate Christmas, knowing the facts about its Egyptian antecedents, that the stories are simply redactions of the ancient past? The birth narratives are literary vehicles that carry a universal truth, and this is their value for us today. There are no second-class citizens in the kingdom that Jesus sought to create. The teachings of Jesus underscore the value of every person. No longer are we to make judgments based on a person's sex or sexual preference. No longer will the Christian church be a fraternity designed to keep women in their place. In Christ there is no separation between people based on the basis of race or creed. The Christmas story is significant for its inclusion of people of all races and creeds. The wise men were Persians, probably of the Zoroastrian religion. The in-clusion of the shepherds in the story speaks strongly of the inclusive nature of the Jesus message, which is no class sep-aration.

The birth narratives carry a message of hope and an-ticipation associated with the birth of a child, which is seen as an opportunity for the peaceful preservation of our plan-et. Pablo Casals captured this idea in the following:

> "Each second we live in a new and unique moment of the universe, a moment that never was before and will never be again. And what do we teach our children in school? We teach them that two and two make four and that Paris is the capital of France. When will we also teach them what they are? We should say to each of them: Do you know what you are? You are a marvel. You are unique. In the entire world there is no other child exactly like you. In the millions of years that have passed there has never been another child like you. And look at your body—what a wonder it is! Your legs, your arms, your cunning fingers, and the way you move! You may become a Shakespeare, a Michel-

angelo, and a Beethoven. You have the capacity for anything. Yes, you are a marvel. And when you grow up, can you then harm another who is, like you, a marvel? You must cherish one another. You must work- we all must work—to make this world worthy of its children."[150]

There is a certain magic to Christmas that need never be lost, as long as we remember that Jesus rejected the notion that miracles proved the truth of his message. For him faith based on miracles is no faith at all, and so faith in miracles isn't faith but fantasy. The trend to precision is always bound up with the trend to amplification. The magic of Christmas must always be tied to our willingness to suspend the rational part of ourselves. Stuart Wilde writes in *Miracles*: "Because the universal law is indestructible; and, therefore, infinite, we can presume that whatever power was used by miracle workers in the past must still be available today."[151] We need to remind ourselves of the words of Jesus on his own miracle making: "He that believeth in me, the works that I do shall he do also; and greater works than these shall ye do."[152]

Somewhere deep within you, you know that you have this kind of power. Even though you may not have an inkling of how to use it, or how to begin to tap into it, you still know that within each of us is a divine, invisible presence that has something to do with creating a state that can only be described paradoxically as "real magic." Real magic thinking says: "I believe it, I know it, and I will access my spiritual powers to do it." Since the magic is the creation of the mind of humankind, we can recapture the spirit of this season any time we wish through our imagination. Just as physicist David Bohm proposes that this world is a projection of events in a deeper realm of reality, William Blake agrees with these poetic words: "All that you behold, tho' it appears Without, it is Within, in your Imagination, of which this World of Mortality is but a Shadow."[153]

A *Course in Miracles* tells us that a miracle is a matter of perception and a matter of our choice. That's the reason I can lose myself in the Christmas carols, singing words that I know are not factual, but words that represent a deeper truth about me and my world. I can still allow the little child in me to come out and play. I can choose to rekindle the flame of ecstasy rather than choosing to be gloomy over the holiday season. Where there is great love, there are always miracles. Miracles rest not so much upon faces or voices or healing power coming to us from afar off, but on our perceptions being made finer, so that for a moment our eyes can see and our ears can hear what is there about us always.

# Chapter 17
# EXPERIENCE VERSUS EXPLANATION

"We may hope that the dawn of reason and freedom of thought in these United States will do away with this artificial scaffolding, and restore to us the primitive and genuine doctrines of this most venerated reformer of human errors."
Thomas Jefferson, Letter to John Adams

The story of Isaiah, the young priest of Israel, is a perfect example of the juxtaposition between experience and explanation. The account is found in Isaiah the sixth chapter, where the young priest has had an experience with God. Being a writer, he attempts to write about his experience. This is the point where words begin to fail, as they always will. He describes the awesome event as if it were some magic show. One would have difficulty duplicating that experience. We can learn several things from this passage. First, getting to know Divinity is to enter into mystery. At the heart and soul of life is mystery. We don't have to manufacture it by creating a script for our "hard to believe" religious dramas. There is a mystery at the heart of the universe. Jesus describes the connection with God as mysterious and compares it to the results of wind which "blows where it wishes and you have heard the sound of it, but do not know where it comes from and where it is going."[154]

At the heart of every experience of God, man has emerged with a proclamation. The proclamation is at the heart and soul of every religion, especially Christianity. The early church proclaimed the observation that God was in

Jesus in some momentous and mystical way. It is only when we move beyond that proclamation, with the explanation, that we seem to complicate the event. Sometimes the experience is so profound that we are driven by the need to explain it and that may have value, but the explanation should never be a substitute for the real thing. It is easy to confuse the explanation for the experience. That is what we have done with the Bible. It was intended as a book to lead us into our own experience with God. Instead, it has become a substitute for that experience.

The priests of the early Christian movement were the people who experienced the presence of God, and then they proceeded to coach others to make the same connection. As years passed, some leaders were not willing to do the work required to make this sacred connection and priesthood became priest-craft. When this happened, the position of the priest became a position of power designed to control the people. The Bible became less and less a map of the terrain that led to God and became a repository of another person's experience, which ultimately became canonized as dogma. When this occurred, the priest became a reformer, instead of a transformer. They were interested in the masses conforming to their religious formulas.

It did not take very long for this process to become corrupted. Notice the development of the priest-craft in Hebrews: "Wherefore, holy brethren, partakers of the heavenly calling, consider the Apostle and High Priest of our profession, Christ Jesus."[155] The Jesus of History wanted only to be our coach, to teach us how to connect with God as Jesus did. The explanation of how Jesus connected with God became so corrupt that we cannot recognize who he was by wading through the Christian scripture much less by wading through Christian tradition. God has never been alien to life; and yet, some might conclude, from reading Christian scripture that He was absent before Jesus was born. One writer had Jesus saying, "All who came before me were thieves and robbers."[156]

We also learn from the Isaiah passage that experience carries with it a mission. Listen to him say, "Here am I, send me." We have interpreted that verse as a call to foreign missions. For Isaiah, he meant that he would become a writer, a spiritual coach leading the Israelites into a transformational experience of God. A religious explanation is designed to motivate followers to desire and seek an experience to which the explanation points. The explanation seeks to map out the spiritual terrain. The only way we can have such an experience is to "walk the path." You cannot make the journey by studying the map. Since the territory is ever changing, you cannot rely completely on maps designed by people in the past, no matter how accurate those maps were then. History has shown that the "priest-craft" has actually discouraged the exploration of the spiritual territory by the laity. In fact, as time moves on, the new generations must create new maps to describe an ever growing and changing experience of the power and presence of the Divine in human life and seek to create a new priesthood that will share their personal experience of that reality. Since the Bible is a pre-scientific document, we cannot take those words as explanation of experience and make them fit a post Copernican world.

The priesthood is not limited to the professional few who have been ordained by religious elite, but the priesthood is available to anyone who desires this role and is willing to pay the price that qualifies them to teach the path. One cannot teach that which one has not experienced; however, one can teach that which one is experiencing. The proper order is essential. First, it is experience that is followed by explanation. No explanation is literally true. We need to touch the experience and then find a way to translate that experience into the language that our generation will understand. We should always remember that our explanations must be limited to the words that we choose to describe any transformative event. Our explanations should always point to the experience that we had of the sacred reality that we call God. An explanation, even if it is in the Bible, can never be a substitute for the real experience. When our explanations are being challenged by new knowledge, we have a tendency to think that our God is being challenged. Since our Bible is an explanation of an experience with God, we can use those words to lead us to our own experience of that reality. When we do, we can write our own Bible. Just remember, it will be just as fallible as the ones that preceded it.

In an abandoned, bombed-out house in Germany at the end of World War II, Allied soldiers found a testimony to faith and the spiritual quest scratched into a basement wall in the Cologne Concentration Camp by one of the victims of the Holocaust.

I believe in the sun
even when it is not shining
And I believe in love
even when there's no one there
But I believe in God
even when he is silent
I believe through any trial
there is always a way.
May there someday be sunshine
May there someday be happiness
May there someday be love
May there someday be peace...."

When He does not speak, we have to speak for Him, just as the writers of the Bible and other Holy Books did in the ancient past. This speaking will always be our experience of that reality that we call God.

# Chapter 18
# FROM SOMETHING THAT DOESN'TWORK TO SOMETHING THAT DOES

*Christianity neither is, nor ever was a part of the common law.*
*Thomas Jefferson*

There is an incongruity found in the history of American "Christianism" that reveals an attempt to impose the ancient laws of Israel on the American community. Ancient Judaism and Islam share one thing in common besides radical monotheism. They celebrate(d) the value of the state or nation over the individual. The individual existed and exists for the sake of the larger group of which they are a part. Both Ancient Israel and Islam are theocracies. America, from its inception, was created as a republic where the individual was of supreme value and the states existed to support or defend the rights of the individual. The Ten Commandments and the 613 laws of Israel were designed to control the individual within the ancient state of Israel, just as Sharia Law is designed to control the individual within Islam countries. These laws are not applicable to citizens of a free state where the individual is the measure of all things. Instead of religion acting as a support system for the individual, it has become a suppressor of the individual for the perpetuation of the institution by demanding individual subservience.

Christians often make the claim that the Ten Commandments are the foundation of American law. This is not correct. This fraudulent claim is so old that Thomas Jefferson felt obliged to refute it in an 1814 letter to Dr. Thomas Cooper. The U.S. law draws its foundation from the common law of England which was firmly in place two hundred years before Christianity arrived there. Only the three seemingly universal human prohibitions of perjury, theft, and murder are part of U.S. laws, but not because of the Ten Commandments. He ended his letter to Thomas Cooper with these words, "Finally, in answer to Fortescue Aland's question as to why the Ten Commandments should not now be a part of the common law of England? We may say they are not because they never were made so by legislative authority, the document which has imposed that doubt on him being a manifest forgery."[157]

The Ten Commandments have been recognized as the basis for Christian morality by the Christian Church since the fourth century. Morality is defined as accepted rightness, imposed by authority figures, determining that which is right for the individual within a given society. Is there any place for rules that are designed to control? Yes, in the infancy of society they were necessary. Moses had to deal with a motley and rebellious group of Jews. What better way to control people than to tell them that God gave the commandments? So the prohibitive statements of ancient Israel had some value in bringing the group into a cohesive whole that provided some boundaries for their behavior. It is much like the boundaries that we provide for our children, but we remove the training wheels once they grow up. The Israelites were much like children in their need for such boundaries. These guidelines were given at the level of their ability to comprehend, accept, and follow.

Have we grown beyond the level of these rebellious religious children? Evidently not! What level of growth have we achieved as a result of the advent of Christianity? Christianity claims to be a superior and unique religious system, yet the positive contribution of its message has been minimal. Many writers have observed that sin has not diminished, nor has warfare lessened as a result of the impact of Christianity on society. America, considered to be a Christian nation, has a pattern of one war every thirteen years in our history. What other nation in the world has this dubious distinction?

It is the thesis of this chapter that "thou shalt nots" never have and never will work. History attests to this observation. The myth of the Garden of Eden teaches us this supreme lesson. God said to Adam and Eve, "Thou shalt not eat." They did anyhow and they died. If Adam and Eve broke the rules and everybody since then has broken the rules, then what are rules for? Consequences do not seem to be a deterrent to bad behavior. Negative commandments do not seem to work. The Garden Myth has a powerful message: "people act from their reactive nature," instead of from a proactive, conscious response based on self-reliance. The couple in the garden was living their lives backward, which is a great definition of evil (live). The proper sequence of living is intuition, thinking, feeling and action. The couple in the garden acted, then they felt the consequences of their action, then they thought "I shouldn't have done that," then they got in touch with God for a correction to that action. Again, consequences do not act as a prophylactic for breaking the law. Penalty does not act as a deterrent to crime. If rules do not work, then why is a society proliferating rules on a daily basis? It is based on an attempt to control behavior, not guide behavior.

Jesus called for his followers to move to a new level of living, beyond morality. His teachings call us to a new dimension of meta-morality or that which is higher than morality. In this new way of living we learn to live out of the internal direction of a compass that is connected to our internal divinity. Jesus identified this ideal person as a "kingdom man." Jesus' message about this kingdom provides a new understanding of a method of conduct based on this internalized principle, which Emerson called "self-reliance." The ethic of this kingdom was one where falseness could not be accepted. Authenticity is then the hallmark of the kingdom person who possesses all the foibles of being human without allowing those foibles to define them. Only an internal ethic, an ethic of consciousness, is fit for a real religion.

To live under the laws of external prohibitions is to create the pretender, which Jesus called the Pharisee or hypocrite. Jesus pointed his finger at these moral fabricators, who designed rules for others to follow, but from which they felt exempt. The unfortunate history of Puritanism has been a commentary on American religious leaders who think they are above the very sins that they loquaciously condemn. Jesus spoke very clearly against this mindset. He was opposed to living life in a box that was defined by the Pharisaical mindset of rules, regulations and restrictions. The greatest delusion of our day is the belief that we can solve the problems of our lives by an ethic of obedience to law. When we confront the person within us for whom the external law was designed, we deal with that part of us which made the Ten Commandments necessary. This self-confrontation is painful, since it brings about recognition of the propensity for the same kind of behavior which exists within us that we otherwise would condemn. This is the meaning of Jesus' words about non-judgment. Jesus' ethic was a radical morality that requires a change in personality, described by John as "rebirth." Life in this kingdom works by the self-imposition of values based on mutual respect for self and others. It is life lived by the Golden Rule. When we implement this standard, we are living by the meta-morality of Jesus which is based on love.

There is a major difference between man-made laws and universal laws. One cannot break the universal laws with impunity. Gravity is an example of a universal law. We teach our children to respect the law of gravity. After they have fallen several times, they learn the lesson and learn to respect this universal law. Through the process of learning what doesn't work, our children develop a healthy respect for heights. They learn to develop personal guidelines based on a developing self-reliance. They learn to define what is best for them, based on discovering what works for them instead of depending on information provided by an outside authority figure.

The Ten Commandments, as a whole, are irrelevant for our day, simply because they do not reflect the higher ethics of Jesus' teachings. The Jesus ethic is one that the Christian Church purports to follow but obviously does not. These ten rules are irrelevant because they do not work and because they do not deal with a higher morality that has an internal reference point. Only six of Moses' Ten Commandments deal with how one human should treat another. Is this really sufficient material for a moral code? Still, many Americans insist that the Ten Commandments are the foundation of our legal system. Some make their claim that the founding of the U.S. Constitution is primarily based on the influence of the Ten Commandments and a belief in God. The term "creator" mentioned in the Declaration of Independence is a generic reference to the "Deist God of nature," not to the Yahweh of the Hebrew Bible. Readers are encouraged to read Thomas Paine's *The Age of Reason* to understand Deist attitudes toward the Bible. The Constitution and Bill of Rights are the foundational documents of our country and contain no religious references. Though the authors of these documents, James Madison and Thomas Jefferson, were Deists, they understood the dangers of mixing church and state. They deliberately and thoughtfully made this country secular favoring no religion. There is no democracy or constitutional law in the Bible; it is based on a theocracy and makes no room for freedom or individualism.

Are the Ten Commandments a valid model for Christians to follow? I will examine each of the Ten Commandments in the light of the Jesus model and let the reader be the judge. Jesus did not give us a list of negative behaviors that the follower should emulate. His eight Beatitudes were affirmative statements portraying a life lived from within. Attempts to use a prohibition to control the behavior of a society usually fail. This is witnessed by the prohibition period in America's attempt to control alcohol that created the crime syndicates of the 1930s and the dramatic failure of the war against drugs in our day. This has led, recently, to several conservative politicians calling for the legalization of drugs in an attempt to limit their use. This argument admits that people in any society will behave the way they wish, especially if addicted, but legalization would eliminate the drug lords and create revenue to pay for the enforcement of the limits to these laws. Such limits to the legalization of alcohol include an outlaw of sales to minors, which had a degree of success. At least the laws make it a little more difficult for minors to purchase alcohol. There are several economists who view escalation of prohibition as the wrong response; they see drug prohibition as the cause of the violence.

The Ten Commandments are the governing rule of Judaism along with 613 other rules, which had the aura of the absolute will of their deity, Yahweh. A belief in a divine source of ethic enforced by the power of God is a concept that has limited appeal in our society, except among fundamentalists. In fact some of the rules of Judaism are downright immoral, especially those that call for severe punishment for minor crimes. It is much like Sharia Law in Islam. These codes were not considered to be universal, since they applied only to the Jews within Judaism. They did not seek to control the behavior of the Jews toward their neighbors, and quite often exempted them from ethical behavior toward non-Jews.

There are actually three versions of the commandments in the Hebrew Scriptures: Exodus 20:2-17, Exodus 34:12-26, and Deut. 5:6-21. The version in Exodus 20 is the most commonly cited. Some scholars have charged that the Hebrews adopted these laws from the pre-existing Code of Hammurabi, which is on display in the Louvre in Paris. These codes were cast in stone circa, 1750 BCE. The Code of Hammurabi has elements of contract law, various human rights, and was considered so fundamental that they even applied to the king. The codes included prohibitions against lying, theft, and murder – rules which are so universal that there are few cultures without them.

The first commandment contradicts the Christian dogma of the Trinity, since the first commandment was strictly monotheistic. No amount of religious double talk about three in one can negate the evidence of this conclusion, since the Council of Nicaea made Jesus equal to God. If Yahweh is the only God, as this commandment implies, then why is Yahweh so concerned about the worship of his competitors? If he is the only God, then the others simply do not exist; there is no need for exemptions.

The second commandment is an extension of the first commandment with an emphasis on the prohibition of graven images. Of course, the Catholics couldn't have built those magnificent cathedrals with their hundreds of statues, relief sculptures, demonic rain spouts, and stained glass windows had they understood the second commandment to prohibit graven images of things in heaven or beneath the water or earth. It is obvious that the early Christian Church did not take this commandment seriously.

The commandment about the name of God is relevant, but it has nothing to do with the phrase, "God damn it," as most people interpret this rule. This phrase may be inappropriate and insensitive language, but it is not a violation of the third commandment. The name of God was shrouded in mystery, so much so that the Jew could not pronounce it or write it. They used substitute names, such as Adonai, Elohim, and El Shaddai. In Jewish thought, a name is not merely an arbitrary designation or a random combination of sounds. The name conveys the nature and essence of the thing named. It represents the history and reputation of the being named. The most important of God's Names is the four-letter Name represented by the Hebrew letters, Yod-Hei-Vav-Hei (YHVH). It is often referred to as the Ineffable Name, the Unutterable Name or the Distinctive Name. Some people render the four-letter Name as "Jehovah," but this pronunciation is particularly unlikely. The word "Jehovah" comes from the fact that ancient Jewish texts used to put the vowels of the Name "Adonai" (the usual substitute for YHVH) under the consonants of YHVH to remind people not to pronounce YHVH as written. A sixteenth century German Christian scribe, while transliterating the Bible into Latin for the Pope, wrote the Name out as it appeared in his texts, with the consonants of YHVH and the vowels of Adonai, and came up with the word JeHoVaH ("J" is pronounced "Y" in German), and the name stuck. I share this information with my Jehovah Witness friends whenever they drop by for a visit.

The Catholic third commandment is to remember to keep holy the Sabbath day. Jews and Protestants call this the fourth commandment. If this commandment is valid, today, then the Seventh Day Adventists are the only sect in Christendom which does not break the fourth commandment. Mind you, there is ample justification for worshiping on Sunday, since it is the day of Jesus' resurrection, but it does not correlate with the fourth commandment. Technically, the Adventists are correct. Until the 2nd and 3rd century most Christian groups kept the Jewish Sabbath. When worship is seen as the organization of one's life around the principle of God's presence in our lives, the question about which day we worship is meaningless. All days have equal importance. It is important to note that the original commandment was a work prohibition and called for a day of rest. The orthodox Jews and the Adventists are the only groups which follow the letter of this law. Technically speaking, the rest of us break the fourth commandment every week.

The fifth commandment links the first four commandments with the remaining five. Commandments one through four are about our relationship with God. Commandments five through ten are about our relationship to our fellow man. It is good for one to honor one's parents, but if the parents deserve no honor, the act is a charade. This commandment makes no provision for a parent who abuses children and, therefore, deserves no honor. Maybe all the parents in Judaism were honorable.

The Ten Commandments of Israel did not apply to non-Jews; so the sixth commandment was limited to the Jewish community. It was O.K. to kill non-Jews, but it was not O.K. to kill each other. Was it wrong for the Israelites to kill and utterly destroy the inhabitants of the Promised Land?[158] Was it wrong for Saul and his army to kill and utterly destroy the Amalekites, including every man, woman, infant and suckling?[159] Why was Saul punished for his disobedience to God in not killing them all? Was it wrong for David to kill Goliath, a man who defied the God of Israel?[160] Was it wrong for Phinehas to take a javelin and thrust it through an Israelite man and his heathen lover, killing both of them with one piercing blow?[161] Was God angered or pleased by this killing?[162] Were other lives saved because of this killing?[163] Was it wrong for Elijah to kill hundreds of the prophets of the false god BAAL?[164] Was it wrong for the congregation of Israel to kill a man who gathered sticks on the Sabbath day?[165] These are just a few Biblical references to show that Israel did not apply the 6th commandment to non-Jews.

Scholars are thrust into a dilemma over this commandment since it has broad reaching implications, especially regarding war. There has been an attempt to justify the acts of war by an analysis of the words, kill and murder. This distinction is spelled out by the following comparison. The word "kill" in Exodus 20:13 and Deuteronomy 5:17 mean "murder." The proper translation is THOU SHALT NOT MURDER. It is interesting that in Matthew 19:18 the KJV correctly translates the Sixth Commandment: "Thou shalt do no murder." The Hebrew word *(ratsach)* and the Greek Word *(phonen⬜)* which is used in the Sixth Commandment both clearly mean "murder." This is a great justification for the millions of people who have been killed in the 13 major wars in which America has been engaged since our creation as a nation. This does not mitigate the psychological damage done to our soldiers, who live with the consequences of this dilemma imposed by a church that taught them, in their youth, not to kill.

The seventh commandment has little to do with marital fidelity. The seventh commandment has to do with a violation of man's property. The prohibition against adultery never included men in the Jewish culture. Women were chattel and second-class citizens in Judaism, just as they are in Islam today. They were even separated from men in the synagogue, as they are in the Mosque today. One wonders about the absence of a man in the story about the adulterous woman brought to Jesus. The man never seemed to be responsible, simply because this rule did not apply to him. The repression of sexual energy has never worked, especially if it is imposed from an outside authority, such as the church or the state. Only an internal discipline that channels this energy has the power to transform the individual into a citizen of the kingdom that Jesus introduced.

That things can be stolen implies a right to own property. The eighth commandment is one most of us can agree has universal application. There are so many ways to steal that we will not attempt to catalog them in this book. The writer of the book of Ephesians writes, "Let him who stole steal no longer, but rather let him labor, working with his hands what is good, that he may have something to give him who has need."[166] The ninth commandment reflects the title of my book, "Thou shalt not lie." If this commandment has validity today, then the church is guilty of breaking this commandment, big time. Breaking this commandment is what this book is all about.

Covetousness implies desire. Desire is not only appropriate; it is God breathed, which is the meaning of the word. It is the abuse of a good thing that poses a problem in the tenth commandment. Desire becomes corrupted when it becomes greed. The story of King David and Bathsheba is a classic example of desire that has been corrupted with tragic consequences. It is to be noted, that the liberation of the natural person is not liberation to license but to consciousness, which is the theme of Jesus' teachings. The ethic of the kingdom requires that all sides of human nature are to become conscious. The key to the ethic of the kingdom that Jesus taught is not obedience, but rather a conscious awareness of when we are hurting ourselves or someone else. When we are forced to live under the religious authority of prohibition, we move rapidly into hypocrisy. We find ourselves living life in a box, defined by others or by restrictions. This was certainly true of the Puritans, who had a major negative impact on the moral climate of America, especially during the 19th and 20th centuries. The Ten Commandments are all stated negatively; it is thou shalt not, and thou shalt nots never work. Not one time is the idea of love mentioned in the Moses Code, which is the essence of Jesus' teachings.

In the Gospel of Matthew,[167] Jesus repeated five of the Ten Commandments, followed by the commandment he called "the second" commandment.[168] The first and greatest on his priority list was the commandment of loving God.

"And, behold, one came and said unto him, Good Master, what good thing shall I do, that I may have eternal life? And he said unto him, Why callest thou me good? there is none good but one, that is, God: but if thou wilt enter into life, keep the commandments. He saith unto him, Which? Jesus said, Thou shalt do no murder, Thou shalt not commit adultery, Thou shalt not steal, Thou shalt not bear false witness, Honour thy father and thy mother; and, Thou shalt love thy neighbor as thyself." [169]

The model that works is found in Jesus' teachings in the Sermon on the Mount and the Beatitudes. This is the model that prompted Jefferson's Bible which included these verses exclusively. Jesus teaches that there is a Pharisee in each of us. Recognition of this fact is the only way that we can overcome the falseness of our personality. Only the genuine self is a candidate for the kingdom of heaven, a topic that is the subject of Jesus' teachings found in the Synoptic Gospels. When we rip away the masks that we have been wearing, we expose that which has been hidden, and that must be addressed and removed according to Jesus. Identification with these outer masks effectively excludes us from the kingdom and produces the hypocrite that has plagued Christianity from its inception. To identify with our mask is to think that we are the person we pretend to be.

The Sermon on the Mount contains the key to mankind's happiness. It is the Golden Key that unlocks the door to life's meaning and fulfillment. It covers all the essentials. It is practical and personal. Once the true meaning of the teachings of Jesus has been grasped, it is only necessary to apply them faithfully in order to get immediate results. If you really want to have prosperity, complete health, peace of mind and spiritual development, Jesus shows us how in these teachings. Jesus calls us to develop attitudes that reflect our being, who we really are.

Of all the strange figures that appear in the Gospels, John the Baptist is one of the strangest. John the Baptist's message tells us what to do. The message of Jesus in the Sermon on the Mount begins by telling his disciples not what to do, but what to be. This sermon can be truly called the Be-

Attitudes. Jesus is speaking of what a man must be, what he must first of all become in himself. He is speaking about inner transformation, inner change, which must come first. John the Baptist placed a great deal of emphasis on external forms, observations and discipline. This is the understanding of the harsh, literal truth, the understanding of the external man. With the message of Jesus we have the inner message, the spiritual or metaphysical interpretation of life's inner meaning.

The children's story *Winnie the Pooh* is a powerful teacher. When one reads A.A. Milne's story, we learn the "how of Pooh." Benjamin Hoff asks us to consider *The Tao of Pooh*. We know some of the characters in the cast. There is Christopher Robin, Tigger, and the Horrible Heffalump. The author has this to say about the characters: "While Eeyore frets and Piglet hesitates, and rabbit calculates and Owl pontificates...Pooh just is." Hoff continues, "When you work with the Wu Wei, you have no real accidents. Things may get a little odd at times, but they work out."[170]

You don't have to do things when you live by the Pooh way. Things just happen in the right way, at the right time. At least they do when you let them. If you're in tune with the way things work, then they work the way they need to, no matter what you may think about it at the time. Later on you can look back and say, "Oh, now I understand. That had to happen so that those things could happen, and those had to happen in order for this to happen." Then you realize that even if you'd tried to make it all turn out perfectly, you couldn't have done better; and if you'd really tried, you would have made a mess of the whole thing. This reflects the teachings of Tao. It means that Tao doesn't force or interfere with things, but lets them work in their own way, to produce the results naturally. Then whatever needs to be done is done.

The Beatitudes is a general summation of the entire teachings of Jesus. He does not commence by saying,

"You must do this" or "Thou shalt not do that." The old order taught men what to do, but Jesus showed them how to be and how to think. He outlines for us a series of attitudes of being, or states of mind, clearly promising definite results that follow certain inner changes. The Be Attitudes begin with the word "blessed." It means "to confer prosperity upon or to enrich". "Blessed" is a one-word definition of all the good that will come to you if you understand and live by these amazing attitudes of BEING.

Charles Sheldon wrote a classic novel entitled, *In His Steps*. This story tells about a community of people who resolved to meet all of life's experiences by asking the question, "What Would Jesus Do?" The more appropriate question is "How did Jesus Think?" To think like Jesus means to experience the power of readjusted mental attitudes. When we learn to do this, we will understand and live by the amazing attitudes of BEING. Second, it means to recognize the power of thought. The very word *man* comes from a Sanskrit word which literally means "to think." Jesus was the pioneer of the soul. He realized that the bridge between man and God is man's thoughts and attitudes.

In the Sermon on the Mount, Jesus tells us about the molding power of our own thoughts. His object was to change thought. When we learn to change our thought about things, we learn to change the whole experience. Jesus was the Master of the situation because He was master of His own thoughts. He kept Himself in tune with the Infinite. Remember, things may happen around you, and things may happen to you, but the only things that really count are the things that happen in you. We become the master of the situation when we become the master of our own thoughts. We can't always control what happens to us, but we can control what we think about what happens in our life at any particular moment. Wouldn't it be great to learn to think as Jesus taught us to think?

# Chapter 19
# "OLE-TIME RELIGION" HAS FAILED

"Rogueries, absurdities and untruths were perpetrated upon the teachings of Jesus by a large band of dupes and importers led by Paul, the first great corrupter of the teaching of Jesus."
Thomas Jefferson

Is there any indication that the religious establishment is accepting the overwhelming evidence that is presented in this book as a motivation to re-evaluate their untenable position? The following words of Oliver Wendell Holmes provide a clue. These words, uttered in 1830, obviously had little effect upon the prevailing religious climate in his day in spite of its profound religious significance. Here is a paragraph from Holmes' review of the first edition of Sir Edwin Arnold's famous poetic account of the life of the Lord Buddha, *The Light of Asia*:

"If one were told that many centuries ago a celestial ray shone into the body of a sleeping woman, as it seemed to her in his dream; that thereupon the advent of a wondrous child was predicted by the soothsayers; that angels appeared at this child's birth; that merchants came from afar bearing gifts to him, then an ancient saint recognized the babe as divine and fell at his feet to worship him; that in his eighth year the child confounded his teachers with the amount of his knowledge, still showing them due reverence; that he grew up full of compassionate tenderness to all that lived and suffered; that to help his fellow-creatures he sacrificed every worldly prospect and enjoyment; that he went through the ordeal of a terrible temptation in which all the power and evil were let loose upon him, and came out conqueror of them all; that he preached holiness and practiced charity; that he gathered disciples and sent out apostles to spread his doctrine over many lands and peoples; that this 'Helper of the worlds' could claim a more than earthly lineage and a life that dated long before Abraham was, of whom would he think the wonderful tale was told? Would he not say that this must be another version of the story of the One who came upon our earth in a Syrian village during the reign of Augustus Caesar and died by violence during the reign of Tiberius? What would he say if he were told that the narrative was between five and six centuries older than that of the Founder of Christianity? Such is the story of this person. Such is the date assigned to the personage of which it is told. The religion he taught is reckoned by many to be the most widely prevalent of all beliefs."[171]

These words were obviously about the Buddha, but it seems that the more evidence one presents, the more it is ignored or vigorously denied by the fundamental community. Just this week I saw an episode of the 700 Club where they were offering a course, "Why is Christianity Unique?" At the same time they were trying to raise $250,000. They were spending all that time and energy on trying to prove something against which all the evidence stands. One is inclined to ask, is it all about money and protecting that funding base?

"Christianism" created a dichotomy between the polar opposites, making the dark side evil and something to be avoided. This split has caused serious psychological conflict in the Christian adherent, creating an internal schism that has had tragic consequences. This is one of the reasons why the church has been so anti-sexual. Instead of embracing the dark side and allowing the spiritual connection to transform it into positive energy, the church has continued to identify sex as the enemy. The beloved theologian-physician-musician-humanitarian Albert Schweitzer believed that the stratagem of bringing the world to Christ through Jesus has failed and needs to be abandoned. He believed that the historical foundation of the Christian faith (as these were laid down by ancient, medieval, and modern thinkers) no longer exists. He would agree with my thesis that there is a need to return to the paradigm that places divinity at the heart and soul of the human being and uses religious giants such as Jesus to lead us in this process of spiritual growth. This would lead us in an application of these principles in practical living. Using Schweitzer's idea, you do not bring anyone to the Christ; you assist others in releasing "the imprisoned splendor" that is innately present in all humans.

The Danish philosopher, Soren Kierkegaard, addressed the central issue of traditional Christianity. He suggested that there are two ways to be fooled. One is to believe what isn't true; the other is to refuse to believe what is true. The traditional paradigm that has embraced an exclusive understanding of grace and the atonement has been shattered by the evidence presented from antiquity. Grace has been highjacked and distorted by Christian fundamentalists to mean being saved by the blood of Jesus for the remission of sins, as expressed in the original lyrics of the hymn, "Amazing Grace." This song identifies humanity as wretches, not merely sinners. The only way for "wretches" to escape the consequence of their sinful state is to embrace a gospel of salvation. Grace, in this context, is something that is dispensed or withheld by the power brokers of religion, which is usually the church. This process ranges from the sacraments of the Roman Catholics to "a profession of faith" or "walking down an aisle" by the fundamentalists.

Grace is actually the foundation of our being on which we stand. It is to the human as the water in the fish bowl is to the goldfish. It is that environment in which we move and live and have our being. Grace is unfettered; it needs no justification. It needs no channel through which it is dispensed. Grace is not a transaction to make; it is a gift to receive. We do not need to develop a doctrine in which this grace is contained, for it cannot be contained any more than atmosphere can be contained. It is free and not conditioned on our "accepting Jesus as our personal savior." This means that there is no plan of salvation, as the fundamentalist prefers to preach. It is tempting to take something simple and mold it into something complex; this practice has been the tradition of Pauline Christianity from the first century.

The history of Christianism has been one written with this complex molding. The physicist, John Wheeler (1911-2008) presents an understanding of just how beautiful a simple idea can be, such as the simple message of Jesus. He suggests that everything must be based on a simple idea. Once we have finally discovered it, it will be so compelling, so beautiful, that we will say to one another, yes, how could it have been any different? This simple truth is to be found in the teachings of Jesus.

Kirby Godsey, Chancellor of Mercer University, has written a delightful book entitled, *Is God a Christian?* He created a firestorm in the South,especially among the Southern Baptists by publishing this book. In this book Godsey challenges the fundamentalist's notion that Grace is exclusive when he writes, "We are all ultimately children of grace. Grace means that our hope does not rest in the affirmation that we believe in God. Our hope rests in the reality that God believes in us. God believes in us more than God believes in our religions. God's unconditional embrace transcends all of our religious systems. God's love is the antecedent of, not the consequence of, our following Jesus or our faithfulness to Allah or to Yahweh."[172]

Chapter four in his book is an expose of the errors of Fundamentally which, incidentally, is a "Johnny come lately" in the Christian community, dating back to the 18th century C.E. He identifies several themes that are characteristic of fundamentalism in all religions, including Christianity, Judaism and Islam. These themes identify this perversion of Jesus' teachings as a form of religious devotion, that has turned in on itself. He says:

> "Instead of trusting God, fundamentalists trust their religion. Their goal is to establish the superiority of their position, religious or political, by gaining ascendancy and defeating their challengers. Fundamentalists, Christian and Muslim alike, are in a war to win the world. Jews in Palestine are in a war to establish the integrity of their holy land. The only way to be sure that we are God's favored people is to defeat those who believe otherwise. In doing so, we destroy those who are infidels, thereby demonstrating that we are favored by God. Religious faith falls victim to the demonic desire to control......Fundamentalism is nothing less than religious idolatry."[173]

Like Godsey, I grew up in a fundamental Southern Baptist home. As a child, I sang songs that made grace conditional thereby turning a rejection of grace into something to be feared. This fear raised its ugly head when one refused to accept this grace on the church's terms. Fear is the weapon of those who wish to maintain power and control. Fundamentalism is woven from the same fabric whether its cloth is labeled Christian, Jewish or Muslim. Meet a fundamentalist and you meet a person who has all of the answers, claiming to possess absolute truth. On this certainty stands his/her security.

I distinguish between a gospel of grace and a gospel of effort. Jesus knew nothing about the gospel of grace as defined by the Apostle Paul. Pauline grace always presupposes a giver and a withholder. The church has been the purveyor of grace according to their rules, and they withhold according to their discretion. But living in a state of grace is not something that is dispensed based on accepting a belief system. The implication of fundamental Christianity is that this grace is not operative unless the dispenser (the church) chooses to find you worthy or demands that you accept some arbitrary theological formula that allows this grace to work. Jesus did not talk about God's grace; he talked about the kingdom of heaven. Jesus said that the kingdom of heaven was to be taken by effort. When Jesus talks about taking the kingdom by effort, he is talking about a process of making it work in daily life, thus producing a transformative experience represented under the image of rebirth. Jesus did not use words such as power and force, but the distinction is present in his teachings. Power is that which is inherent in our status as children of God; while force is external manipulation of our will by those in control. It is always the same whether it is in religion or politics.

Physician and author, David Hawkins, makes a distinction between power versus force in his book by that title. Hawkins is a psychiatrist who practices healing modalities through assisting the patient by enhancing the power and level of consciousness through greater integrity, understanding, and compassion. Much of his book is devoted to the process of making the simple obvious. He proposes that if we can understand even one simple thing in depth, we will have greatly expanded our capacity for comprehending the nature of the universe and life itself. The religious elite love force; the evolving spiritual pilgrim embraces power. Control over others is not an expression of power. It is the abuse of power. Thought is your formed power and the word is your spoken power, which becomes manifest. When you use power, you are literally shaping and forming the conditions in which you live. You can change your environment and your world by simply changing your thinking. If you permit thoughts to be formed which are of extremely high frequency, such as love, wisdom and understanding, you create a very spiritual atmosphere. Prayer has been defined as giving spiritual radiation treatments. It is specific thought forms moving in your mind for perfect resolutions. You are actually radiating low spiritual frequencies that will adjust and alter the consciousness of the person for whom you are praying. Of course, you are automatically bene-fited when you allow yourself to be used to this end. Such power moving through you allows you to become a chan-nel through which God's power is expressed. When you learn to live in this consciousness, you accomplish so much more with less effort. You end up doing less on the outer but affecting more. Additional information about this book is found in my notes.[174]

Ole time religionists speak of salvation in terms of "find-ing God." How can something be found that was never lost? How can you lose that "in which you live and move and have your being?[175] A better metaphor than "being lost" is "sleep." This is the metaphor that George Gurdjieff uses in his writings. I was introduced to the teachings of George Gurdjeiff by a Unity teacher, Ed Rabel. The Gurdjieff writing is an entire work built around the idea of waking out of our spiritual sleep. This work stands as a seminal treatise about the value of effort and focus in one's spiritual quest. A British psychiatrist, Maurice Nicoll, has written a commentary of five volumes on Gurdjeiff's work. In these volumes, the mo-tif is based on work. It takes effort to hone the spiritual life. It is not the simplistic announcement of the Apostle Paul, who preached salvation by pronouncement; it is the rec-ognition that one must "take up his cross" and follow the teachings of Jesus. It takes no effort to believe in a religious system, especially one that pronounces you whole with no effort. We seek to answer the question as to why funda-mental Christianity is so popular in America, today. The an-swer is simple. It requires nothing from you. It is salvation by grace, according to Paul. It is the gift of God, not of works. This does not square with the teachings of Jesus, who held people personally accountable for their behavior. Remember his words to the woman taken in adultery- "go and miss the mark no more." To paraphrase Jesus, "stop sabotaging yourself and learn to stand on your own economic feet, not on your back."

A study group in Sarasota, Florida, spent four years studying the works of Gurdjieff using commentaries by Maurice Nicole on Gurdjieff's writings. Gurdjieff's teaching is called the fourth way. It is a way of life, just as Jesus' teaching is a way of life. Listen to him speak: "Religion is doing; a man does not merely think his religion or feel it, he lives his religion as much as he is able, otherwise it is not religion but fantasy or philosophy."[176] Gurdjeiff refers to the human condition as waking sleep. It is a self-deceptive state of the human being that achieves much, but accomplishes very little. Gurdjieff believes that only one thing is necessary for humans to awaken out of this sleep. It is necessary for individual men and women to awaken by remembering who they are, and then to become who they really are, to live it in the service of this Truth. Without this awakening and this becoming, nothing else can help us. But it is very difficult to accomplish. An extraordinary quality of help is needed. To this end, Gurdjieff created what has come to be called "the Work." This idea is reflected in his book entitled: *Life is Real Only When I Am.* Gurdjieff uses the phrase "self-remembering" as a means to connect with the internal master, which he believes is the real self. The Gurdjieff work remains above all else, essentially an oral tradition, transmitted under specially created conditions from person to person, continually unfolding, without fixed doctrinal beliefs or external rites, as a way toward freeing humanity from the waking sleep that holds us in a kind of hypnotic illusion.

Gurdjieff taught that alone, by oneself, an individual can do nothing. That is the reason why the group is preeminent in his community. To be able to work in life in the full sense would be considered a very high achievement. The struggle to be "present" in everyday life constitutes a major aspect of Gurdjieff's teaching, a struggle which leads to a full engagement in the duties and rewards of human life, now and here. In this context, Gurdjieff created conditions to help his pupils experience the fundamental practice of self-observation. Through such an experience, a man or woman can begin to come into contact with an ever-deepening sense of inner need which allows an opening to a powerful conscious influence within oneself. According to Gurdjieff, without a relationship to this more central aspect of oneself, everyday life is bound to be an existential pris-on, in which the individual is held captive, not so much by the so-called forces of modernity, as by the parts of the self which cannot help but react automatically to the influenc-es of the world. The help offered by the special conditions of the work is, therefore, understood not as replacing our life in the world, but as enabling us, in the course of time, to live life with authentic understanding and full participa-tion. I have a more detailed explanation of this teaching in my notes at the end of this book.[177]

An understanding of Jesus' teachings on the kingdom of heaven is the key to internalizing these concepts in our personal lives. We will possess the key to his teachings if we understand what he meant by the phrase, "the kingdom of heaven." That this phrase is the master key to his teachings is apparent when we count the number of references in the Gospels to this phrase. It is found thirteen times in Mark, the first Gospel, thirty-eight times in Matthew, twenty-eight times in Luke and only once in John; however, the phrase "eternal life" is substituted for this phrase in the Fourth Gos-pel. Fifteen of the parables of Jesus are directly concerned with the kingdom of heaven (God), with these parables being introduced by the phrase, "the kingdom of heaven is like." Notice that Jesus does not say, "The kingdom of heaven is." Jesus always used images or symbols since he was dealing with mystery. For example, he said in the Syn-optic Gospels, "Because the mysteries of the kingdom of heaven are revealed to you, but they are not revealed to them."[178] Jesus taught that the kingdom of heaven was an inner spiritual reality, not something imposed on you from without, such as an edict of a church. The kingdom is not something coming upon us from outside ourselves, but is a reality within ourselves. Nor is the kingdom a set of moral rules imposed from outside by an all-powerful church but rather, a self-regulating compass that allows us to internalize these teachings for proper conduct in daily life. Jung speaks of the "shadow," that part of human personality that makes external rules necessary. If we lived by the teachings of Jesus, we would not have to depend on these external rules for our conduct. We would have the ability for inner confrontation and correction which would produce a higher morality than that produced by adhering to the Ten Commandments. For most people a commandment is something to be broken. History supports this observation.

The kingdom person is one who has experienced a new life that is so radical that it amounts to a complete change and renewal of personality. Paul alluded to this change when he said, "If any man be in Christ Jesus, he is a new creature, old things are passed away, behold all things have become new"[179] The only problem here is that Paul was talking about a belief system, while Jesus was talking about an experience that established a higher spiritual and psychological consciousness. Fundamentalism has followed Paul and not Jesus on this issue since salvation is reduced to accepting a propositional statement about Jesus and has little to do with following his teachings. This cheap grace of fundamentalism actually produces a sentimental religion that is based on believing. In order for something to be real; it must be heartfelt, because real religion must touch our emotions as well as our intellect. Since the kingdom of heaven deals with hard spiritual facts, there is no room for religious sentiment which is characteristic of "ole time religion."

Dietrich Bonhoeffer was a very exceptional person, a Lutheran clergyman who challenged Hitler publicly (even returning to Germany after having escaped for a time first to England and then to America). The Nazis arrested him in 1943 and Himmler himself ordered him hanged in April, 1945, just a few weeks before the allied liberation of his concentration camp. His insightful book, *The Cost of Discipleship*, survived the Nazi book burnings. His idea of "cheap grace" explains not only the hollowness of German Christianity but that of American Christianity as well. Although I do not agree with Dietrich Bonhoeffer's salvation theology, I resonate with many of his statements concerning "Cheap Grace" which he writes about in his book. He admits to the errors of his church when he writes: "We Lutherans have gathered like the eagles around the carcass of cheap grace, and there we have drunk of the poison which has killed the life of following Christ"[180] Obviously, he meant to say "vultures" instead of "eagles", but the idea is still powerful.

Although the Roman Catholic Church hasn't suffered as much as fundamentalist Protestant churches from the "cheap grace" syndrome, it does suffer from a very similar problem, which might be called "cheap sacraments." An example of cheap sacraments is the belief that its priests have the power to wipe sin out with a mere sign of the cross over a penitent confessor and the mumbling of the words: "I forgive you, in the name of the Father, the Son and the Holy Ghost." Bonhoeffer refers to "cheap grace" as grace sold on the market like cheapjacks' (sic) wares. "This cheap grace has been no less disastrous to our own spiritual lives. Instead of calling us to follow Christ, it has hardened us in our disobedience. Having laid hold on cheap grace, they were barred forever from the knowledge of costly grace. Deceived and weakened, men felt that they were strong now that they were in possession of this cheap grace— whereas they had in fact lost the power to live the life of discipleship and obedience."[181] What Bonhoeffer means by "costly grace" is linked to his understanding of vicarious (substitute) atonement as the channel through which God's grace is dispensed. It is this idea that is challenged in this chapter, which is the major distinction between Jesusonian Christianity and Christianism/ Pauline Christianity/ Orthodox Christianity. Grace is not grace if it costs anything. It is the gift of God.

"Ole time religion" has put Jesus in a straitjacket by insisting that one believe in him in order to "be saved." Not all members of the ole time religion cult are accepting of each other, nor do they adhere to the "plan of salvation" as presented by the apostle Paul. Just recently I read the personal account of a major New Testament scholar, who was a student at Moody Bible Institute. When he left that school to attend Wheaton College, another evangelical institute, the concern was voiced by the Moodyites that the people at Wheaton may not be "real" Christians. According to them, real Christians speak in tongues. Real Christians have been "born again, according to our interpretation." Real Christians know how to genuflect. Real Christians believe the same theology. Real Christians attend the right church. Real Christians have been baptized in the proper manner. Real Christians use the same language, sprinkled with pious phrases. It is this narrow-minded exclusivity that has given Christians a bad name.

The fundamental Christian community is so hungry for a validation of their unsupportable theology that they have latched on to an erstwhile quarterback named Tim Tebow as their evidence of God's imprimatur on their brand of Christianity. In the fall of 2011, the young, charismatic football player had some incredible instances of success that bordered on the miraculous. In one game he gained 316 yards, and his 31.6 yards-per-completion statistics proved more than coincidence for these fundamentalist Christians. That these same numbers were the same John 3:16 that he wore under his eyes, was non-controvertible proof that Tebow's success was due to divine intervention. When well-meaning supporters of a particular religion latch on to a figure whose success validates their belief, they are open to the proverbial "egg on your face." Since Tebow's performances were inconsistent, as his horrible stats and errant passes attest, a football player's victories and heroics are no place to look for Christianity's vindication. Those who have a mature faith remind us that God's presence is not something that waxes or wanes with the fortunes of a football player or any other evidence of God's will at work.

South Carolina has been called the buckle of the Bible Belt; so why was a presidential candidate booed when he invoked the Golden Rule as a means of dealing with our foreign policy? The occasion for booing was a comment by Texas Congressman Ron Paul about respecting the sovereignty of other nations when it comes to bombing. His comment in context was: "My point is that if another country does to us what we do to others, we are not going to like it very much. I would say that we maybe ought to consider the Golden Rule in foreign policy. Don't do to other nations what we don't want them to do to us. We endlessly bomb these countries, and then we wonder why they get upset with us." This reaction to Paul's suggestion is a prime example of "Christianism" abandoning the teachings of Jesus for a more expedient path, one that panders to the war-mongers. If I remember correctly the Golden Rule is a key part of original Christianity and all other major world religions. Jesus refers twice to this principle where he said "Do to others whatever you would have them do to you. This is the law and the prophets."[182] Whatever happened to "ole time religion" in the South? Or, is what we are seeing in this debate really "ole time religion" in action?

Using the early teachings of Jesus as the fulcrum, we have a standard by which we are called to live as exemplified by Jesus. Of this way Jesus said, "Straight is the path and narrow is the way that leads to eternal life and no man puts his hand to the plow and looks back."[183] The language of Jesus was written in the flesh of human experience. The words must become flesh if they are to have any meaning for us. The principles must be followed, if they are to transform human consciousness. The explanations that follow this experience are always secondary. To be a member of the Jesus pathway implies that we seek to study these teachings and to live up to them. When we fail, we simply try again, using the failure as feedback information to improve our effort. We don't have to ask, "What would Jesus do." We already know that what he taught is what he would do. We have his teachings. We have his life. We have the blueprint. All we have to do is read this blueprint and follow it.

"Ole time religion" has greatly inhibited the spiritual growth of the individual by insisting that he/she accept a surrogate for the process that once led the initiate to spiritual transformation. This is the abstraction of the indwelling Christ within man, and externalizing it in one man, Jesus of Nazareth. This reduces mankind to the level of pitiful supplicant. The dis-empowering language of Christianism is quite revealing with words such as surrender and acceptance. It is because Christianism has taught that man is sinful, that he has behaved badly which is the result of self-fulfilling prophecy. Quite often this was done under the cloak of the very religion that sought to save them. Kuhn concludes: "History shows no evidence whatsoever those men have been less sinful, less afraid of death, or more loving and generous in life since the advent of Christianism."[184]

This leads us to a re-examination of the concept called the atonement. This doctrine has been unfortunate for humanity in that it robs man of his own divine initiative and reduces him to a spiritual beggar. The word atonement, constructed from "at" and "one," means "to set at one" or "to reconcile." In Christian Theology, atonement denotes the doctrine of the reconciliation of God and man accomplished by the Crucifixion and death of Jesus Christ. There have been three major theories of atonement: the ransom theory, the Anselmian theory, and the Abelardian theory.

- The ransom theory, first propounded by Origen (c. 185—254), was developed from Mark 10:45 and explained the atonement as a price paid by God in Christ to the devil. He used a grotesque analogy of a fisherman, with Jesus being the bait that God used to catch the devil.
- St. Anselm (c. 1033—1109) explained the atonement as an act of satisfaction paid by Christ as man to God, who demanded from man perfect obedience to the law, which he could not fulfill because of his sinfulness.
- The exemplarist theory of Peter Abelard (1079—1142) viewed Christ's death as an inspiring appeal of love evoking in the sinner a response of love, thus removing his sin.

Orthodoxy is threatened by a new understanding of Jesus' life and death which leads us to a re-examination of this basic element of redemption, called the atonement. This was the interpretative myth on which "Christianism" was built. One can either accept or reject this concept of redemption according to what one regards as binding evidence. The early evidence was derived from an internal source (Paul's writings) created about the crucifixion by the early church, which constitutes its dubious claim of uniqueness. It is completely void of any external evidence such as the support of secular history, which is completely silent on the subject. Viewed in terms of salvation theology, the orthodox interpretation of the crucifixion has led to movements, causes, and all sorts of discords, whose results have generated extreme intolerance, war and persecution.

Carl Jung has astutely observed the danger of a sub-stitute religion in the following paragraph: "The Imitatio Christ" will forever have this disadvantage; we worship a man as a divine model embodying the perfect meaning of life, and then out of sheer imitation we forget to make real the profound meaning present in ourselves. If I accept the fact that a god is absolute and beyond all human experi-ence, he leaves me cold. I do not affect him, nor does he affect me. But if I know, on the other hand, that God is a mighty power within my own soul; at once I concern myself with him."[185]

Back in the 90s we invited John Shelby Spong as a guest speaker to our church at Sarasota, Florida. We rent-ed the large Methodist Church in downtown Sarasota and prepared for a huge turnout. We were surprised when a contingent of Methodist ministers from nearby Bradenton showed up with picket signs denouncing him as a heretic. Jack went outside and invited them to come in to hear him speak because he suspected that many of them had not read a single book he had written. He handled the con-frontation with a sweet spirit that characterizes a man who is comfortable with an appellation that would previously have led to his being burned at the stake.

Bishop Spong presents a clarion call for Christianity to change or die. In his book by this title, he reminds us that the traditional interpretation presents us with a strange im-age of God. He contends that human beings are neither perfect nor fallen; they are simply incomplete. He calls for recognition of and a willingness to grasp the fullness of that humanity. He challenges the creedal doctrines of the Chris-tian faith and claims that they are simply not true. These creedal doctrines, according to him, have captured the life of Jesus inside the symbols of a dying theism. He recom-mends that we seek a new way, a totally different way to tell the Jesus story that is our only option. It is simply a return to the original story of Jesus as a God presence, who lived what he taught, which ultimately resulted in his death. The success of our reformation lies in our ability to rescue Jesus from theism without destroying the power of the meaning that was found in his life.[186]

He addresses one of the main contentions of my book that Paul was not correct in his claim that God was in any way "reconciling us with God." Early Christianity was merely a radical, transforming, boundary-breaking religious experience. Jesus turned the values of his day upside down. He called people to follow in his path. One of his main points is the claim that Jesus stood on the side of marginalized members of his society. He sees the cross as an ultimate portrait of the power of love.[187] We are beginning to have a dawning realization that Jesus is different from others only in degree, and we are called on to close that gap between us and him. This is the idea found in the words of Jesus when he said, "And greater things will you do than I."[188] He also called us, "gods."[189] This is a passage from which I have never heard a sermon. I spoke about this in detail in chapter five.

How does prayer fit into this religion-less Christianity that I and others are advocating? Prayers are made in some fashion by every religion on the planet and to some extent it is the center of their focus; e.g., the Muslims who pray five times a day. Prayer is the most abused and misused word in religious language. The Aramaic word for prayer is *slotha*. It comes from the root word *sla*, which literally means "to trap" or "to set a trap." Thus, prayer in its initial sense implies "setting your mind like a trap so that you may catch the thoughts of God"—in other words, "to trap the inner guidance and impulses that come from your inner spiritual source." In Aramaic the word *slotha* carries other meanings such as these: "to focus," "to adjust," "to incline," and "to tune in." Rocco Erricco suggests a modern analogy for our understanding. If I were going to speak to you in Aramaic and ask you to turn on the television set to a particular channel, I would have to use the Aramaic root word *sla* for prayer. And it would mean "to select the proper channel," "to adjust the set," or "to tune in the desired program."[190]

In prayer, we are adjusting and preparing our minds and hearts to receive God's program. It is our fears that create blockages that hinder our connection with our Source. So prayer becomes an "attuning process" where we eliminate everything that is not the proper station that we are seeking. God (spiritual forces) is always broadcasting and televising. Spirit is constantly beaming, sending, and signaling to everyone and everything in creation. It is our responsibility to "set a trap for God," which suggests that we trap all the love, joy, truth, peace, energy and compassion we need when we are receptive to all which is rightly ours. This kind of prayer qualifies us to receive God's provision and in turn to express gratitude and thankfulness. To use another analogy, genuine prayer prepares the mind to become a blank tape ready to receive all the good that we may need in our lives. When our minds are free, open, clear and sensitive, we can trap the power and presence of God. Spiritual forces are always available to work with us, if we are trapping and working with the universal program and not just acting out of our own egos and agendas. Prayer does not deal with a capricious God; it is a technique for achieving unity with God.

Now that we understand prayer as "setting a trap for God," let's take a quick look at the Aramaic meaning of the term, "God". The Aramaic term for God is *alaha*. In Arabic it is *allah*, and in Hebrew *elohim* or *alohim*. All these words for God derive from the same Semitic root—*al* or *el*. The Aramaic root means the helper, the supporter, the one who sustains. Another Aramaic term for God is *ithea*, "self-existent," "self-cohesive and sustaining." The self-existent principle known as *ithea* in Aramaic is the creative presence and power that abides within us. *Ithea* is the force within and behind the universe that keeps everything on the move.

A spiritually devout Easterner would say, "God is my very breath, my very heartbeat, and my life". The Hebrew psalmist understood this when he said, "As the hart pantest after the water brook; so my soul panteth after thee, O God."[191]

We can learn to move with God through the power of prayer. Through prayer we learn to "tune in" to all the good there is. When we are attuning our minds with the proper attitudes, we are "setting a trap for God." In other words, prayer is connecting with our Source. Jesus' method of prayer is a simple and direct acceptance of the good the universe has for us. There is really no secret about communing with the innate spiritual forces that reside in us. Our job is to let go of ideas that are stumbling blocks and hindrances to us. Jesus taught his disciples a new way of praying because he knew certain things that they did not know. He knew that human beings do not have to beg and beseech God to give them the good things of life, as if God would not otherwise have done it. In prayer we need to understand that all good in the universe is always present for us. God has given everything that we as humans may need for our well-being. Jesus also knew that our capacity to receive good is limited only by a restricted realization to claim and accept it. The purpose of prayer, then, is to affirm in our consciousness that which is true of God and of our relationship with Him.

Eric Butterworth emphasizes this idea with these words, "Prayer is not something we do to God but to ourselves. It is not a position but a disposition. It is not flattery, but a sense of oneness. It is not asking but knowing. It is not words but feeling. It is not will, but willingness"[192] Man's dilemma is that he has become trapped in a religion of propositional theology and the correlate dilemma is thinking that prayer is manipulating God. Jesus addressed this issue and the art of prayer in his Sermon on the Mount. I quote from this text in its entirety:

"Be careful not to practice your righteousness in front of others to be seen by them. If you do, you will have no reward from your Father in heaven. So when you give to the needy, do not announce it with trumpets, as the hypocrites do in the synagogues and on the streets, to be honored by others. Truly I tell you, they have received their reward in full. But when you give to the needy, do not let your left hand know what your right hand is doing, so that your giving may be in secret. Then your Father, who sees what is done in secret, will reward you. And when you pray, do not be like the hypocrites, for they love to pray standing in the synagogues and on the street corners to be seen by others. Truly I tell you, they have received their reward in full. But when you pray, go into your room, close the door and pray to your Father, who is unseen. Then your Father, who sees what is done in secret, will reward you."[193]

In his classic essay, "Self-Reliance," Ralph Waldo Emerson addresses the idea of prayer from a new perspective when he says:

"Prayer looks abroad and asks for some foreign addition to come through some foreign virtue, and loses itself in endless mazes of natural and super-natural, and mediatorial and miraculous. Prayer that craves a particular commodity, anything less than all good, is vicious. Prayer is the contemplation of the fact of life from the highest point of view. It is the soliloquy of a beholding and jubilant soul. It is the spirit of God pronouncing His works good. But prayer as a means to affect a private end is meanness and theft. It supposes dualism and not unity in nature and consciousness. As soon as a man is at one with God, he will not beg. He will then see prayer in all action."[194]

Jesus never said, "Pray this prayer" when he gave us the model prayer that we call "The Lord's Prayer." Jesus had no thought of giving us a rote prayer that would be repeated with little meaning in either song or verse. He was telling us "how" to pray and not "what to say." The English word, prayer, came from the Latin, *precari*, meaning "to beg." Instead of spelling it "pray," they should spell it "prey" for that is what most people are doing. They are attempting to prey on God, or get from God, what they want. If the Lord's Prayer is read as an affirmation, it is then consistent with the teachings of Jesus about God. The Lord's Prayer, in The Aramaic, is a beautiful rendition of this affirmative theme. It is presented below as a comparison to show the original along with an English translation, faulty as it may be.

Avvon d-bish-maiya, nith-qaddash shim-mukh.
Tih-teh mal-chootukh. Nih-weh çiw-yanukh:
ei-chana d'bish-maiya: ap b'ar-ah.
Haw lan lakh-ma d'soonqa-nan yoo-mana.
O'shwooq lan kho-bein:
ei-chana d'ap kh'nan shwiq-qan l'khaya-ween.
Oo'la te-ellan l'niss-yoona:
il-la paç-çan min beesha.
Mid-til de-di-lukh hai mal-choota
oo khai-la oo tush-bookh-ta
l'alam al-mein. Aa-meen.

Matthew 6:9-13
Our Father who is everywhere,
Let your name be set apart
Come your Kingdom (counsel)
Let Your desire be, as in the universe,
Also on the earth
Provide us our needful bread from day to day.
And free us from our offenses, as also we have freed our offenders.
And do not let us enter into temptation,
But separate us from error.
For belongs to You the kingdom, the power, and the song and praise.
From all ages through all ages.

In contrast, the prayer as it is translated from the Greek implies a pleading mentality. It seems to say: "Please give me," "Please forgive me." "We beg you not to lead us into evil." If we continue to insist that the Gospels were originally written in Greek, instead of Aramaic, we will continue to get these faulty translations. It is amazing to me why many scholars continue to defend the Greek over the Aramaic versions in the ongoing controversy. Maybe it's because they were trained in the Greek and not the Aramaic and we prefer to stay with that which is familiar.

An Interpretation From The Aramaic by dr. michael ryce:

Our Eternal Creator, parent to us all, who is in the realms of the unmanifest, make a space in us for wholeness that we may be taught to honor, EMULATE and serve You.
Let Your counsel, Your wisdom and Your Love come alive in us, let Your Light penetrate us...Attune us to and empower us to conceive of and understand that Will which You have already created for us. Teach us so that we may give birth to Your fruit.
That You renew and feed us daily with the presence of Your Love, the Love of each other and the food we receive is a gift we gratefully accept! Thank You for restoring us to abundance, teaching us gratitude and how to give as you give and present Love as you are the Presence of Love, for both the just and the unjust.
That You forgive from us those realities we have engaged in that do us harm and do not belong in our humanness is another of Your blessings we appreciate...we commit to responsibility and forgiving as to those painful realities others trigger in us.
When we are tempted or lost in materialism or fall out of harmony with Your Love, that You are there with us - Being the space of Love, that Your Love is always Present no matter how far we fall—no matter where we go, is a blessing we gratefully accept.

That, with your grace, You deliver us from our errors and through Your light part us from darkness is another blessing that flows from Your Presence.

We receive each of these gifts with gratitude and praise.

Sealed in Trust, Faith and Truth, AMEN[195]

# Chapter 20
# THE CHARADE OF THE SECOND COMING

"It is between fifty and sixty years since I read it (i.e. the Book of Revelations), and I then considered it merely the ravings of a maniac, no more worthy nor capable of explanation than the incoherence of our own nightly dreams."
Thomas Jefferson Source: Letter of Thomas Jefferson to General Alexander Smyth, Jan. 17, 1825.

I normally would not address a topic as bizarre as this, if this belief system were not such a threat to our existence as a planet. Just as I would try to dissuade a child from jumping off a barn in anticipation of flying, I try to quench the zeal of those who burn with the fervor of apocalyptic fire. This belief affects a large number of people, potentially the entire planet, even those who do not embrace it. This is due to the nature of self-fulfilling prophecy. Prior to the eighteenth century, the Bible was not interpreted with the apocalyptic slant of today's armchair theologians. Today, *rapture, Armageddon, tribulation, and millennium* are household words thanks to writers like Hal Lindsey, Tim La-Haye and Jerry Jenkins. Lindsey developed a theory based on the belief that the events found in the Book of Revelation are describing historical events of our own day. Usually these have something to do with the re-establishment of the nation of Israel in 1948. In his book, Lindsey took a passage from Revelation that implied that the end of the world would come within a generation of "the blooming of the fig tree." Israel in the Hebrew Bible was often referred to as a tree so Lindsey took this to mean that within a generation after the founding of the nation of Israel the Second Coming would occur. He wrote the book, *The Late Great Planet Earth*, based on this theory and sold a lot of copies before history proved him wrong. Originally predicting that the world would end in 1973, Lindsey was not deterred and simply he revised his prediction to the year 1988. Although the accuracy of these predictions appears flawed, it has not slowed the constant flow of connecting these prophecies with current events.

The kind of writings that spawn these fanciful theories is called apocalyptic literature. The word apocalypse is a Greek word that means "an unveiling, the disclosing of something that has been hidden." I have found very little clarity and disclosure in this form of literature. The two best known of the apocalyptic literature are Daniel in the Hebrew Bible and The Book of Revelation in the New Testament. Both of these writings contain dubious material that was slow in universal acceptance by even the religious communities that spawned them. The book of Daniel was written in B.C.E. 195, many years after the Hebrew Canon was essentially closed. There was a group of writings that came from this period called the Apocrypha, which is generally rejected by a major part of the Christian community. Most Protestants consider these books to be spurious. This rejection includes that portion of the Christian community who considers the book of Daniel to be the source of important predictions about the end of the world. The material found in Daniel is the same kind of material found in the Apocrypha. It is material that requires careful interpretation because it was written in cryptic language. I am amazed at the creative interpretations that emerge from the book of Daniel and other apocalyptic literature. The bizarre theories that germinate from apocalyptic writings originate from a literal mindset that insists that every word of the Bible is infallible.

A sample of the material that is written by the fundamental religious community is couched in the form of fictional novels such as *Left Behind*. This book has sold several million copies and was made into a movie. The premise of the novel is based on a pre-millennial interpretation of the "Second Coming of Jesus." The author conceived his idea of fictionalizing an account of the rapture and the tribulation, while sitting on an airplane and musing what would happen if the Second Coming would occur and the pilot was a Christian. For the sake of the "unsaved" passengers one would hope that the co-pilot was also an "unbeliever." Notice that all these theories presuppose a formularized religion that determines the outcome of the individual's fate at death or the second coming.

If it were not for the fervency of the apocalyptic believers, we could dismiss these theories as preposterous and move on to more practical matters of faith and practice. However, many of those believers gleefully anticipate a conflict between the Jews and Arabs, which they view as a prerequisite to the second coming. These deluded thinkers support any political decision that moves us closer to World War III. Instead of fearing such a war, this group welcomes it and lobbies for its fruition. When you have radicals in the Muslim religion who support a jihad and radicals in the Christian religion who anticipate an Armageddon, you have the ingredients of a conflagration awaiting the right torch. Both sides are convinced that God supports their position. That has always been the danger of religion, a point of view that insists on being right at other's expense. In this case the fate of the world is weighed in the balance.

If a conflagration occurs, and I believe it may, it will not be because of Biblical predictions. It will be because of Biblical abuse, both of the Koran and of the Holy Bible. The greatest abuse of Bible interpretation surrounds the Book of Revelation. It is from the Book of Revelation that most of the theories of the second coming are derived. In this book, we find all kinds of bizarre symbolism, which is taken literally by those who frame these scenarios. There is disagreement among the interpreters. There are those who are called pre-millenialists because they believe that Jesus will come before the tribulation and the thousand-year reign.

Those who believe that the rapture will occur after the millennium are called post-millennialists. A minister friend of mine refers to himself as a pan-millennialist, asserting that everything will pan out in the end. One of the greatest misunderstandings of apocalyptic literature believes that the material found in these books refers to historical events of our day or to any period of time other than the one in which it was written. The author of the Book of Revelation was a man named John, who wrote in a time of terrible persecution. These writings describe events that occurred during the reign of the Roman emperor Domitian. Under his reign many Christians were harassed, imprisoned and executed for their faith. John was exiled to an island called Patmos. There he wrote to encourage the remaining Christians to maintain their faith in the midst of persecution. Under these conditions, he had to conceal his meaning by using a code that the Christian community would understand but could not be used as an indictment against them. For example, when he talks about the Great Satan or the anti-Christ it was fairly obvious to his fellow Christians that he was talking about the Emperor. Another example would be the mark of the beast that the followers of Satan would have. Most likely John was simply talking symbolically about anyone who bowed down in worship to the emperor.

I have mentioned two images that loom large in an apocalyptic picture of the end of the world. One is the anti-Christ. Apocalyptomists extract an early picture of the anti-Christ, even before Jesus was born. They reference Daniel[196] as the first reference to the anti-Christ. The anti-Christ "will attack the mightiest fortresses with the help of a foreign god."[197] The anti-Christ has been identified with every major

"evil" personality, since the time of Napoleon. These identifi-
cations include Hitler, the Pope (for anti-Catholics), and the
latest being the attackers of the world Trade Center. The
most recent candidates for the anti-Christ were not Sad-
dam Hussein nor Usama Bin Laden, nor Arafat, but the King
of Syria, Bashar al-Assad, who according to one writer is the
"foreign god" behind the Islamic terrorist organizations. You
can begin to see how convoluted these theories can become. Any attack on the U.S. is seen by these Apocalyptomists as an attack on Israel, since America is considered to
be the foundation and support of Israel. What is happening
in the Middle East today provides more than ample fodder
for the burgeoning scenarios that are emerging from that
section of the planet about the end of the world. The fundamental ministers continue to fan the flame, since these
events vindicate their pre-conceived notions about end
times. Identification of Allah with Satan and Mohammed as
the False Prophet are part of these twisted interpretations,
forcing a contemporary meaning on chapters such as Revelation 13. To this literal mind set, the devil is a literal person
with power that is designed to oppose God. He has power
to possess the physical bodies of those in political power
and to use that power to control the direction the world is
moving, coinciding with Biblical predictions. In other words,
the Bible can be used as a road map to determine the direction world events are moving.

   We have taken a brief look at the Anti-Christ, now on to
the second image, the mark of the beast. The actual "mark"
is Antichrist's name or number, not ours. This image is taken
from Revelation chapter 13. "If anyone worships the beast
and his image and receives his mark on the forehead or on
the hand, he, too, will drink of the wine of God's fury, which
has been poured full strength into the cup of his wrath...
There is no rest day or night for those who worship the beast
and his image, or for anyone who receives the mark of his
name."[198] With modern technology this theory has received

some elaborate identification. Some believe that this mark may be directly linked with a computer chip. Others think that it is associated with the universal pricing codes, those little black stripes that you see on the outside of any package you may buy these days. Those who foster this belief see the mark as a forced identification that one must have in order to buy or sell anything. They use an interesting proof text, "He also forced everyone, small and great, rich and poor, free and slave, to receive a mark on his right hand or on his forehead so that no one could buy or sell unless he had the mark, which is the name of the beast or the number of his name. This calls for wisdom. If anyone has insight, let him calculate the number of the beast, for it is man's number. His number is 666."[199] Proponents who take this number as a forecast of the future are quick to point out that the issue here is that of worship. People must vow their devotion to this worst of all the false Christs by allowing either his name, or else the number of his name to be placed on them in a prominent place as a symbol of their allegiance.

Returning to the bar codes mentioned before, the UPC codes are generally divided into two parts by three bars, one at the beginning, One at the end, and one in the middle. According to this view, these marks may be longer than the numbers but they may look the same as one of the codes for the numbers six. Thus, some bar codes do have the number 666 built into it. Others have suggested that the name Bill Gates adds to 666. They ask, "How did he get so powerful so quickly?" To add to this speculation, Windows 95 adds up to 666. Add a 6 to Phillips 66 and you might find that gasoline is the beast. Route 666 is the way of the beast. I might add that "cute purple dinosaur" adds up to 666. The best possible interpretation for the number is to be found in the historical context of the writing. Since John, the writer of Revelation spoke Aramaic, it is plausible to find that Nero Caesar's name in Aramaic is NRON KSR. Numeric values for these letters are N, 50; R, 200; O, 6; N, 50; K, 100; S, 60 and R, 200 for a total of 666. It is interesting to note that Aramaic, along with Greek and Roman languages, used alphabetic characters to represent numbers. An anonymous author pinned his frustration about this code in the following poem: "This Bible Code," moaned Reverend Dix, "puts my name in a terrible fix. He was fit to be tied when the code was applied, and his name totaled six sixty six."

Those who take these numbers seriously, find no humor in these observations. There is a strong warning that God, in response to an act of disobedience, will disenfranchise anyone who has this mark. This implication removes the eternal nature of one's salvation through the blood of Jesus. It is obviously not a permanent washing, since one, according to this belief, must endure to the end to be saved. Accompanying miraculous signs and wonders will deceive the people who make the eternal mistake of receiving the mark and worshiping the beast and/or his image. The writer of Revelation adds this warning, "But the beast was captured, and with him the false prophet who had performed the miraculous signs on his behalf. With these signs he had deluded those who had received the mark of the beast and worshiped his image. The two of them were thrown alive into the fiery lake of burning sulfur."[200]

The interpretation war continues around this issue between those who believe the Christian will be raptured before this time and those who believe that no one will escape a personal decision regarding the mark of the beast. The appeal is made to the Christian to withstand the offer of the mark. This is accompanied by the promise that they will immediately be in the presence of the Lord in "paradise."[201] This happens after you are obviously killed for disobeying the order to receive the mark. Miracles from Satanic power, this position holds, will deceive many into taking the mark and thereby forfeiting their salvation. All of these things will happen only to those who are the last generation. Your decision at this point will determine where you will spend all of eternity, according to this view. All of these positions are sprinkled liberally with Biblical quotes that support their point of view and are taken totally out of context with the larger text of which they are apart.

Armageddon is a name that rings fear in the hearts of movie goers and Bible readers. It is a synonym for annihilation. The best account of Armageddon is found in Revelation 19:11-21. Armageddon is a battle. It is the battle where God finally steps in and takes over the world and runs it the way it should have been run all along. It is the start of a peaceful and bountiful time known by some as the Millennium.[202] The reason it is called Armageddon is because it takes place in a location called the valley of Megiddo. Armageddon means mount of Megiddo in Hebrew. According to certain views, this battle will happen after God's plan has been completed. A dictator, who heads up a worldwide government, will run the world. This man (also known as the anti-Christ) will rise to power on a wave of world euphoria as he temporarily saves the world from its desperate economic, military and political problems with a brilliant seven-year plan for world peace, economic stability and religious freedom. Although most of the world will initially hail the Beast as a political savior, three-and-a-half years after the enactment of the seven-year covenant, he will revoke the peace pact and show his true colors. He will outlaw all religions, except the worship of himself and proclaim himself savior. The Antichrist's reign will last seven years after which Jesus will return and Armageddon takes place. Notice that there is little agreement among proponents of Biblical prophecy on the order of these events. According to some, Biblical prophecy requires the rebuilding of the Third Temple before the events leading up to the Battle of Armageddon can begin. However, the Islamic holy sites of the Dome of the Rock and the Al Aqsa Mosque currently occupy the Temple Mount in Jerusalem. Some radical Christians want to "liberate" the Temple Mount, rebuild the Temple and make Armageddon possible. This fact underscores how dangerous this point of view can be. "How near is Armageddon?" is a question that only mankind can answer. Whether it comes at all is a choice that we must make. If it comes, it is not due to God's infallible plan for mankind. If it occurs, we will see desolation on the face of this planet that will equal the images found in the Book of Revelation.

The phrase "abomination of desolation" is found in the book of Daniel and has been interpreted as a description of the carnage that would take place at Armageddon:

"And He shall confirm the covenant with many for one week: and in the midst of the week He shall cause the sacrifice and the oblation to cease, and for the overspreading of Abomination He shall make it desolate, even until the consummation, and that determined shall be poured upon the desolate."[203]

What is this "abomination of desolation?" Jesus says in the context, "Look, you asked me what will be the sign of the end. Let me tell you. There will be wars, but that is not the sign. There will be earthquakes, but that is not the sign. Iniquity will abound, but that is not the sign. There will be religious persecution, they will betray you, but that is not the sign. When you see the 'abomination of desolation' spoken of by Daniel, that is it!" The critical question here is, "what did he mean?" Was this a reference to what occurred in the destruction of the temple in C.E. 70 as most critical scholars assert? Or, is this a reference to coming events?

There is exaggerated emotion and excessive fear generated around the topic of the second-coming. The following account would be comical, if it were not so tragic. In Seoul, South Korea, Lee Jang Rim, head of one of some 200 Protestant churches in that country, created national hysteria by announcing that the rapture would take place on October 28, 1992. He urged his followers to prepare for their journey through the skies. Riot police, plainclothes officers, and reporters crowded outside Korean churches, flanked by fire engines, ambulances, and searchlights. In December 1992 Rim was arrested and sentenced to two years in prison for having bilked $4.4 million from his flock. He had invested the money in bonds that didn't mature until 1993.

Among Protestant groups, the Seventh-day Adventists continue to be the most vocal predictors of an impending Second Coming, although they no longer set a date for that event. Jehovah Witnesses have an even worse record of failed predictions than the Adventists. Some believers make a distinction between the rapture and the Second coming. In the rapture, Jesus is coming for the church. In the Second coming, Jesus is coming with his church. In the rapture only Christians will see Him and in the Second coming every eye will behold his appearing. The rapture can happen at any time while the second coming occurs at the end of seven years of Tribulation. In the rapture, the spirits of those dead in Jesus return with him to receive their resurrected bodies; while in the second coming, Christians return with Jesus in already resurrected bodies riding on white horses. The rapture seems to be designed for Christians, while the second coming is for redeemed Israelites and Gentiles which implies a second chance. The rapture contains a message of hope and comfort, while the Second coming is about judgment and wrath. You may have seen the bumper sign, "During the rapture, this car will be unmanned." There is a counter sign that reads, "When the rapture comes, may I have your car?"

This fear-laden topic has captured the attention of poets and play-writers, including W.B. Yeats and Samuel Beckett. When I read Yeats' poem on the Second Coming, I feel the pain that he must have experienced that led him to write such a morbid piece. Beckett, on the other hand, when he wrote his play, *Waiting for Godot* [204] must have been thinking about the Second Coming. There seems to be an implied religious aspect in most Existential literature as they contemplate a society devoid of order, norms, or divine guidance. We are all waiting for something. It's how we fill in the time "until whatever is going to happen happens" that is the subject of the play. With the presence of a dying tree on the stage, Beckett seems to be making the Existential statement that Christianity is empty and dying. To them, God is an empty promise. In the absence of a supreme being, the two main characters of the play, Vladimir and Estragon turn to each other for that role. Only one of the characters acknowledges the presence of a boy on stage, which implies a heavenly visitation. Acting as an interpretive intermediary, Vladimir responds to Estragon's question, "Do you think God sees me?" with the answer, "you must close your eyes." Vladimir and Estragon must find Godot for themselves, because He will never come to them. This is a clear statement of the doctrine of the divinity of the Self, which has come to be expressed by New Thought religious teachers. This is the Existential solution. One writer put it this way: "To exist in a world devoid of reason, one must create that reason, else be doomed to endless years of waiting for enlightenment to come, which it never will, appearing only on the horizon of tomorrow's forever" (Anonymous).

Is the Second Coming a reality on which we can rely? I think not. It is, in my opinion, another lie, told by those who wish to control the masses by fear. We have seen interpreters take passages from Daniel, Thessalonians, the Synoptic Gospels, Corinthians, and the book of Revelation, mix them altogether and "voila" out comes a conclusion that is devoid of reason. Remember, I began this book with the observation that perception determines reality. If God is Unconditional Love, then it is not possible for Him to be vindictive, judgmental and wrathful. These horrible pictures of God are part and parcel of the Second Coming scenario. How you will view the evidence surrounding the rapture, second coming, Armageddon, and the Tribulation will be determined by how you see God. When the prophets made their proclamations, they gave us two scenarios and then encouraged us to make a choice about which one becomes reality. We are standing at the crossroads, and I choose the road less traveled. It is the only road that will bring abiding peace and the willingness to co-exist. We do not have to choose Armageddon, but that is a choice awaiting our decision.

Arthur Findlay has summarized the influence of Egyptian ideology on the Hebrews as well as Christians, regarding this idea of a returning God. "The belief in the return of Christ, which has prevailed throughout the Christian era, is just the descendant of this old belief that the Savior god would return to earth. This return of the Savior was associated by the Babylonians and Egyptians in relation to the sun" (They developed an elaborate astronomical system around this return. The Word "Christ" means the anointed one, thus the Savior-God worshipers looked upon their Savior as the Christ. This word has come down to us from the Greek word Christos, meaning 'the anointed". In all of the countries surrounding the Mediterranean in those days, the Jews alone were without a Savior God, and their comfort came from their anticipation of his coming to earth and reigning over them as god-man. This idea was not peculiar to the Jews, as at least fifteen hundred years before the Hebrews thought of a Messiah, the Egyptians were writing of the coming of a just ruler who would lead the people on the road to righteousness. The Jews evidently borrowed the belief from Egypt, and called this anticipated righteous leader by the name of Messiah, which conveyed to them the same idea as Christos did to the Greeks. He was the expected anointed Jewish King who was to subdue all their enemies, whereas the Christ of the Greeks, and the neighboring nations, was the anointed victim who had suffered on the altar as a sacrifice for their sins."[205]

We have examined a lot of dirty bath water in our evaluation of Christianity vs. "Christianism", but let's be careful not to throw out the baby with the bath water. Jesus has always been a vital part of my life and continues to be important. I have rejected the baggage that organized religion has imposed on him and retained the reality of who he was and what he was all about. Jesus was a way-shower, my spiritual brother and an avatar. He was not the savior of the world and never claimed to be. An interesting verse in the Bible, which gives Peter the papacy, has been misunderstood. When Jesus asked Peter, "Who do men say that I the son of man am?" Peter replied: "Thou art the Christ, the son of the living God."[206] Jesus' response, as traditionally interpreted, makes no logical sense. Jesus responded: "Thou art Peter and upon this rock I shall build my church." Peter knew that his name was Peter. What Jesus was saying is profound. Jesus was saying, "Thou art! Peter" and on this understanding "I will build my spiritual community." Jesus knew nothing about the church as we know it today. He was familiar with the synagogue and Hebrew worship but knew nothing about the elaborate ritualistic and creedal based church that would develop in his name. He knew that the Christ existed in everyone as a potential. That is what he was telling Peter in this passage. It is our responsibility, through work and effort, to make that potential a reality.

The second coming of Jesus will not be the historical Jesus in person, but his form of higher consciousness within us all. For this advent we yearn with expectation and enthusiasm. When people ask me if I believe in the second coming, this is the answer that I give them.

# Chapter 21
# THE FUTURE OF RELIGION

"I like the dreams of the future better than the history of the past."
Thomas Jefferson

What does the future hold for world-wide religion? I wish I could be as optimistic as Longfellow's words in his hymn, "I heard the bells on Christmas Day." I resonate more with his words in the third verse of his poem, when he wrote, "And in despair I bowed my head: There is no peace on earth, I said, For hate is strong and mocks the song of peace on earth, good will to men." As long as America, which purports to be a Christian nation, has a Department of War and Defense instead of a Department of Peace, peace will be an illusion. When we sing "Let There be Peace on earth," we should substitute "love" instead of peace, since love is the pre-requisite of peace. Until we decide to follow the teachings <u>of</u> Jesus instead of believing a teaching <u>about</u> him, we will continue to sink into a religious morose that leads to disillusion. I trust that the internal conflicts that have been the history of "Christianism" will not continue to proliferate with religion separating people from each other within the Christian community.

When we think about the future of religion, we are assuming that religious institutions and ideas are capable of change even though many of them insist that they are the recipients of a final revelation. Today, the world's great religions find themselves at a critical juncture. Adhering to values and beliefs that are often thousands of years old, they are finding it increasingly difficult to provide the spiritual guidance and moral authority necessary to face the challenges of modern society. However, students of religion from Hans Kung to Huston Smith have emphasized the transformations that have been a part of religious traditions over the centuries.

When discussing religious and spiritual issues, I have found it useful to distinguish the two terms. For me, the word "religious" refers to the adherence to an organized system of beliefs about the divine (something deemed worthy of veneration and worship) and the observance of rituals, rites, and requirements of that belief system. "Spirituality," on the other hand, can be thought of as one's focus on and connectedness to a Source (God) believed to be beyond one's full understanding. Any rituals, behaviors, or beliefs that accompany this process are internally generated rather than reflective of an external authority or institution.

As the world chaos grows, fear masquerading as faith will proliferate. We live on guard now as various color-coding systems inform us of the relative toxicity of our air or the degree to which we are imminently at risk of a terrorist attack. Governmental agencies have been created to perpetuate this fear, this anxiety, and this angst. There is a ubiquity of fear prevalent in America today. The marriage of Christianity and fear is not surprising, when one traces the history of apocalyptic religion that has captured evangelical Christianity. This "Religion of Fear" differs from that which preceded it. This form is far more politicized than its predecessors. This religion of fear has permeated pop culture, even reaching into the field of entertainment. A religion of fear has been exacerbated by the *Left Behind* series that tells us as much about the politics of these authors as about their theology. Fear of hell is a major part of the conversion motif found in this series. Throughout this series, the authors delight in representing Christians as outlaws and targets of oppression. This series is pregnant with signs of the end of times.

Religious certainty will be more in demand than ever. The resurgence of religious certainty has deepened our cultural divisions, while political discourse gets more polarized. Complete religious certainty is the real blasphemy of our day. That sense of certainty has even entered democratic politics in the U.S. Mega churches, which preach absolute adherence to an inerrant Scripture. These churches will thrive while moderate churches will decline. Why is this so? Because people in this mindset wish to find comfort in spoon-fed religion and are threatened by an examination of ideas that may challenge their indoctrinated convictions.

Religion will continue to play a superficial role in American culture. There will still be football players praying in the end zones to a God who favors one team over another. Loud voices will be raised demanding that the Lord's Prayer be prayed at these games. Religious leaders will insist that spoken prayer be restored in the public schools of America as a means to restore civility among our young people. We will still evoke God as the defender of our politics, our culture, and our way of life.

There is one bright spot. The religion of the future will be studied by the theologians objectively instead of subjectively. Academic pursuits will not be confined to a defense of the faith by those who profess to seek the Truth. The pursuit of and evaluation of the evidence that defines religion has always been the goal of the scholar and academician. However, most ministers who received a seminary education were exposed to this knowledge, but they learned quickly to ignore this evidence when preaching to their congregation. This is called "job security". Quite often, vested interests of those in authority have limited this quest for truth. The discovery of the Dead Sea Scrolls is evidence of this cover-up. These documents remained the exclusive property of the Roman Catholic Church for almost forty years; thus preventing an unbiased examination of those critical texts by scholars. The church refused to allow access to these documents for fear that they may contain material that would contradict their dogma or challenge their authority.

For your information, the Dead Sea Scrolls are a collection of 972 texts from the Hebrew Bible and extra-biblical documents found between 1947 and 1956 on the northwest shore of the Dead Sea from which they derive their name. The texts are of great religious and historical significance as they include the oldest known surviving copies of Biblical and extra-biblical documents, and preserve evidence of great diversity in late Second Temple Judaism. These manuscripts generally date between 150 BCE and 70 C.E. Before this discovery, the earliest extant manuscripts of the Old Testament were in Greek in manuscripts such as Codex Vaticanis and Codex Sinaiticus. One can see how valuable these documents are to Biblical scholars.

Religion will become more stratified on one extreme and more egalitarian on the other hand. In other words, there will be greater polarization in the religious community. There is a direct correlation between stratified religions and sexual prohibitions. By stratified, I mean males ranking above females who are above children; and mankind ranks above the natural world. In contrast, there are many more sex positive religious cultures found in the Far East. In those cultures, men and women have equal status and the environment tends to be nurtured rather than exploited.

Robert Putnam and David Campbell have co-written a book entitled: *American Grace: How Religion Divides and Unites Us.* In this book, the authors point out the religious polarization versus pluralism that characterizes the American religious life. The question arises as to how religious pluralism can co-exist with religious polarization? The answer is to be found in the Bill of Rights, especially the First Amendment.

Americans are increasingly concentrated at both ends of the religious spectrum, the highly religious at one pole and the avowedly secular at the other. At the same time, they are extremely fluid, learning to adapt and evolve, not only as individuals but also as a part of a group. This adaptation and evolution is our hope for the future.

In the religious world, there are those who predict that the conflict between the Eastern and Western religions will grow with a widening distrust of each other, especially between Christians and Muslims. I wish that I could believe that world-wide Islam was an innocuous and beneficent religion impacting only its adherents, but I have serious reservations. As a practicing religion, I have no issue with Islam. However, the commitment of Islam to Sharia law is my main source of internal conflict and concern since it poses a major threat to freedom. On the other hand, the Christian community appears to continue to talk about love, and continues to practice hate and bigotry. So the question is, "Can the great religious traditions of the world reinvent themselves in order to address the needs and hopes of a complex, materialistic, and an increasingly secular twenty-first-century world?" I would like to think they can, but the jury is still out on this matter.

Religion, as orthodoxy, will proliferate both in the Christian and Muslim world due to an exploitation of women. This is the cause of a major worldwide polarization in religion today. I like to see myself as a tolerant person who accepts diversity as a philosophical idea. However, I have mixed emotions over Islam. As a religion, I see Islam posing no threat to freedom or to the existence of other major religions; however as a political system, it poses a major threat. In Islam there is no separation of church and state; the state is a theocracy. I have a major problem with the law under which a Muslim state operates. Under Shariah Muslim law, the state controls the private as well as the public life of all its citizens, especially the women. In the Western

World (America), Muslim men are starting to demand Sharia Law so the wife cannot obtain a divorce, then he can have full and complete control of her. Radical Islamists are working to impose Sharia Law on the entire world; however, this philosophy permeates the more modern Islamists, even in America. Muslim- American citizens are exempted from Obama's healthcare plan. According to Sharia law, they cannot participate in gambling, since insurance is a form of gambling. American prisons are a breeding ground for Islamic converts who emerge from incarceration radicalized and angry.

It's hard to imagine that in this day and age, Islamic scholars agree that those who criticize Islam or choose to stop being Muslim should be executed. Sadly, while talk of an Islamic reformation is common and even assumed by many in the West, such murmurings in the Middle East are silenced through intimidation and threats of violence. Westerners are lulled into complacency over the threat of radical Islam by a desire to be tolerant and to express a spirit of religious and social diversity. Tolerance and diversity can only exist in a free society. Take away this freedom, and you remove any possibility of tolerance and diversity. While Westerners tend to think in terms of religious people developing a personal understanding of and relationship with God, Sharia Law advocates executing people who ask difficult questions that could be interpreted as criticism.

Some Islamic countries retain laws forbidding defamation of religious belief. Some retain laws forbidding all forms of blasphemy (e.g., Germany, where, in 2006, Manfred Van H was convicted of blasphemy against Islam). This is seen by some, as official endorsement of religious intolerance, amounting to the criminalization of religious views. The connection between intolerance and blasphemy laws is closest when the laws apply to only one religion. In Pakistan, blasphemy directed against either the tenets of the Qur'an or the Prophet Mohammed is punishable by either life imprisonment or death. Apostasy, the rejection of one's old religion, is also criminalized in a number of countries (notably Afghanistan) where Abdul Rahman was the first to face the death penalty for converting to Christianity.

Where Islam is the dominant religion (as it exists in Saudi Arabia, Pakistan and Iran), there is no religious tolerance or religious diversity. The Organization for Islamic Cooperation exists for the purpose of combating religious intolerance against Islam. They have lobbied for 12 years in order to curb the freedom of speech in America in regards to Islam. OIC has consistently argued that criticism of Islamic ideas be treated as illegal defamation. Countries belonging to the OIC include Pakistan, Iran, Saudi Arabia and Qatar. Most notably, these countries adopted the Cairo Declaration in 1990, a declaration which rejected primary principals of the U.N.'s Universal Declaration of Human rights. The Cairo Declaration said that free speech, along with other rights, should be protected as long as it is consistent with Islamic Law. That means that expressions poking fun at the prophet Muhammad or any other element of Islam would not be protected under law. This is consistent with the principles under which Sharia Law operates. If Muslims are able to induce ecumenical attitudes and pluralism in Western Christians, it can prove advantageous for them. You may be sure you will not encounter any reciprocal fair-mindedness in Saudi Arabia, much less in Iran.

What has happened in the United Kingdom in the past ten years has been called the Islamification of Britain. There are those in England who believe that their left-leaning government favors Islam and disfavors Christianity. This charge came from none other than the Church of England, which accuses the government of "deep religious illiteracy." More than 5,000 people in Britain converted to Islam in 2011. That's an average of 14 a day, and most of them were women, including Lauren Booth, Tony Blair's sister-in-law. This is a strange paradox, since Islamic women are treated as second-class citizens in Islam. This corresponds with the growing number of blacks in America who convert to Islam. They are, as one black author observed, reverting back to a plantation mentality surrendering their freedom for an identity that is neither cultural nor religious. The theologian Hans Kung has reminded us that there will never be global peace until there is harmony between the world's great religions, especially Islam and Christianity. But this will never happen while Christians and Muslims claim to hold a monopoly on divine truth.

Public education in Western culture has always been to some extent a "melting pot," but the increasing number of students with non-Western cultural values and religious traditions is causing public school educators to grapple in new and sometimes uncomfortable ways with the challenges such diversity poses. Some of these challenges are practical; e.g., should Muslim girls be allowed to wear burkas and should schools designate only Christian religious holy days as school holidays? The popular pluralistic claim that the beliefs of every religion are an equally valid expression and should be respected is a valid philosophical concept. That is a belief that I embrace. However, this pluralism will work only in a society that respects individual rights and supports the equality of all citizens.

In the future, free people will seek a free religion that celebrates hope and embraces imperfection. These people will seek a faith where practice is more important than theory, love is more important than law, and mystery is seen as an insight into truth rather than an obstacle. New Thought will continue to attract those who are disillusioned with traditional religion. Unfortunately, most people have to wait until they are older for this to happen; thus the tendency for New Thought religious expressions to attract older people. Younger people are either turned off by religion or they are indoctrinated by the system and by parents who subject them to the institutional system.

An anonymous German playwright said it best when he made a simple observation: "If God were to hold all Truth concealed in his right hand, and in his left hand only the steady and diligent drive for Truth, albeit with the proviso that I would always and forever err in the process, and to offer me the choice, I will with all humility take the left hand, and say, Father, I will take this—the pure Truth is for You alone." That sentiment is as true now as it was two centuries ago when this writer wrote it. Except now the very survival of our civilization may depend on it.

Stanley Kripner and Alan Watts have co-written an article on the future of religion with suggestions about how these religions can be productive and positive. "First, these religions need to be transcendental, acknowledging the existence of some process or entity worthy of respect and reverence, whether it is named God, the Goddess, the Eternal Tao, the Ground of Being, or something else. Secondly, the religions of the future need to be embodied; they need to accept and cultivate bodily health, sensual pleasure, and sexual diversity. Religious institutions have a centuries-old record of sexism, homophobia, and rage against the body. The third hallmark of future religions is that they need to be socially relevant and liberating, opposing tyranny and social injustice. Religions of the future need to afford opportunities for sharing, compassion, peacemaking, and the manifestation of love. Finally, the religions of the future need to work with science and not in opposition to the scientific method, scientifically gathered data, and scientifically conceived theories. Science and religion ask different questions; science inquires as to 'how?' while religion queries 'why?'"[207]

These writers hope that the new religions will be a dramatic contrast to the old religions that insist that an idea is either true and revealed, or false and heretical. The religions of the future also need to admit that they are incomplete processes representing a quest that is necessary to inspire and provide consolation for the human species, especially during times when inspiration and hope are rare commodities. This quest is characterized by asking questions, not by giving concrete answers. Unique among nations, America is deeply religious, religiously diverse, and remarkably tolerant. But in recent decades, the nation's religious landscape has been reshaped.

In the future, some religious groups will be open to contributions from other religions. They will be more eclectic and ecumenical. They will learn from each other. From Buddhism, they will learn the value of the inner world as found through meditation. They will also learn the value of detachment. Detachment is the absence of a need to hold on to anyone or anything. It is a life of arriving rather than a life of striving. It is experiencing what it feels like to row your boat gently down the stream. The fewer impediments to the energy flow, the more we harmonize with the energy system called the universe. The third value we derive from Buddhism is the emphasis on universal divinity. According to an old Hindu legend, there was a time when all men were gods, but they so abused their divinity that Brahma, the chief god, decided to take it away from men and hide it where they would never again find it. Where to hide it, became the big question. "Here is what we will do with man's divinity. We will hide it deep down in man himself," said Brahma.

From Christianity, other religions will learn the meaning of forgiveness and love that Jesus taught. This is not a Greek idea, but an Aramaic concept that stressed releasing and letting go, rather than letting someone off the hook. Pierre Teilhard de Chardin identifies love as: "The affinity which links and draws together the elements of the world....Love, in fact, is the agent of universal synthesis."[208] From Islam, the world religions can learn the concept of commitment. This concept is a double- edge sword, since commitment and fanaticism are extremely close. It is to be noted that fanaticism is not limited to Islam, since all major religions suffer from this corruption.

From Judaism, other religions will grasp the meaning of the Hebrew word, *Shema*. God is one and so are we. Break down the word "universe" and you find two words: "uni" meaning one and "verse" meaning song. One song! No matter how we separate into individual little notes, we are still involved in the one song. Albert Einstein wrote these words: "A human being is a part of the whole called by us universe, a part limited in time and space. He experiences himself, his thoughts and feelings, as something separated from the rest, a kind of optical delusion of his conscious-ness. This delusion is a kind of prison for us, restricting us to our personal desire and to affection for a few persons near-est to us. Our task must be to free ourselves from this prison by widening our circle of compassion to embrace all living creatures and the whole nature in its beauty."[209]

I have little hope for change or for the improvement of organized religion in the future since fundamentalism and orthodoxy seem to be more entrenched than ever. How-ever, there is a bright light shining throughout the world in the form of spirituality. This movement is spontaneous, free, and individualistic with little or no organization. It seems to be a fraternity of seekers motivated by the desire to con-nect with God without the accoutrements of that which has defined religion in the past. Sometimes it is a return to ancient practices shared by seekers throughout antiquity, such as meditation and private prayer. In other cases, the seeker is finding new and exciting avenues for this spiritual connection. Long before the development of contempo-rary religions, indigenous cultural groups had developed a repertoire of plants, chants, rhythmic music and movement, self-regulatory practices, and voluntary shifts in psychologi-cal states to produce spiritual and religious experiences.

In my research, I discovered a new word," entheogens," which defines a process of awakening the Divine within. In the past an entheogen is a psychoactive substance used in a religious, shamanic, or spiritual context, such as the American Indian's use of peyote. The word "entheogen" was coined as a replacement for the terms hallucinogen and psychedelic. Hallucinogen was popularized by Aldous Huxley's experiences with mescaline which was published as *The Doors of Perception* in 1954. Psychedelic, in contrast, is a Greek neologism for "mind manifest", and was coined by psychiatrist Humphry Osmond. Huxley was a volunteer in experiments which Osmond was conducting on mescaline. The book, *Entheogens and the Future of Religion* edited by Robert Forte, with rave reviews by Huston Smith and Harvey Cox, presents a well-articulated, thoughtful, and rational basis for understanding the power of psychedelic bio-chemicals to stimulate visionary experience. These essays make a strong case for the use of these substances in future religious practice.

Because of the addictive nature of these controlled substances, I do not believe that they provide the answer for the seeker's inner journey. Stanislav Grof came to this conclusion in his research on LSD at John Hopkins University, where he sought to provide the same results without using a chemical drug. In 1998, he did extensive research with thousands of clients participating in LSD facilitated psychotherapy. He recognized the addictive danger of psychedelic drugs and focused on developing an alternative method, which he called "holotropic breath-work." Grof, a Czechoslovakian psychiatrist, was one of the founders of the field of transpersonal psychology and a pioneering researcher into the use of non-ordinary states of consciousness. The holotropic is characteristic of non-ordinary states of consciousness such as meditative, mystical, or psychedelic experiences. Dr. Grof writes in his book, *Beyond the Brain*, "Western science is approaching a paradigm shift of unprecedented proportions, one that will change our concepts of reality and of human nature, bridge the gap

between ancient wisdom and modern science, and reconcile the differences between Eastern spirituality and Western pragmatism."[210]

The word, "breath", has Jewish roots with one ancient
Hebrew word for God being *ruach*, which literally means
"wind." This wind of God became personalized and we call
it Spirit. This *ruach* was thought to be connected in some
way to human *nephesh* or breath. Breath is a force that
is internal and wells up within us without external stimulus.
In some sense it is identical with life itself. Without it there is
death. There is some evidence that Jesus practiced "breath-
work" with his disciples where it is said, "Jesus breathed on
them."[211] This translation makes no physical or spiritual sense.
Dr. Michael Ryce offers the explanation that in the original
language of the scriptures, Aramaic, the proper translation of that passage is "He breathed them," rather than "he
breathed on them". This translation makes a great deal of
sense.

Dr. Michael Ryce operates a retreat center in the
Ozarks, where he practices still-point breathing, a method
that is used to open the veil of the Temple, the veil that is
developed by holding the breath when one is in denial
and does not want to deal with what is going on inside of
them. Still-point is a method for opening the internalized
patterns that hold one out of spiritual truth and being. An
experience of a return to the newborn state of pure being and love can be achieved through Still-point; and,
over time with its practice, one integrates the true self into
one's life as the fear and the hostility-based false self is dis-
solved. Christ then arrives on earth! Still-point, coupled with
the other tools he teaches, especially the internal oriented
Aramaic process of forgiveness, dissolves the programmed
illusions and delusions of the world and replaces them with
a true spiritual experience, the presence of human life and
love. More information on Michael Ryce's teachings and
methods is available at whyagain.com.

In 1995, I was diagnosed with prostate cancer with a Gleason score of 6.2 and a PSA of 12. I decided to use alternative medical and spiritual treatments in lieu of the standard medical procedures. Sixteen years later, with a PSA ranging between 12 and 177, I am asymptomatic and living a vibrant, energetic life at 78 years. A major part of my treatment was my decision to visit Heartland in the Ozarks for two months for study and spiritual treatment. It was there that I participated in "breath-work." This method provided the space for love to accomplish its healing magic in both psychic and spiritual realms. I had unprecedented inner visual and existential experiences that provided me with a connection with my source (God)) in a profound way. Dr. Ryce continues to use this "breath-work" as a corollary to his workshop on "Why Is This Happening To Me Again" and his book by that same title.[212]

These spiritual seekers share a fellowship of togetherness, but it will not be bound by an organizational or institutional straitjacket. The community of seekers will follow the procedures for building community provided by M. Scott Peck in his book, *The Different Drum*.[213] This book should be mandatory reading for anyone seeking to build a genuine spiritual community. He lists the characteristics of a real community as follows:

- Inclusion, commitment and consensus: Members accept and embrace each other, celebrating their individuality and transcending their differences. They commit themselves to the effort and the people involved. They make decisions and reconcile their differences through consensus.
- Realism: Members bring together multiple perspectives to better understand the whole context of the situation. Decisions are more well-rounded and humble, rather than one-sided and arrogant.
- Contemplation: Members examine themselves. They are individually and collectively self-aware

of the world outside themselves, the world inside themselves, and the relationship between the two.

- A safe place: Members allow others to share their vulnerability, heal themselves, and express who they truly are.
- A laboratory for personal disarmament: Members experientially discover the rules for peacemaking and embrace its virtues. They feel and express compassion and respect for each other as fellow human beings.
- A group that can fight gracefully: Members resolve conflicts with wisdom and grace. They listen and understand, respect each other's gifts, accept each other's limitations, celebrate their differences, bind each other's wounds, and commit to a struggle together rather than against each other.
- A group of all leaders: Members harness the "flow of leadership" to make decisions and set a course of action. It is the spirit of community itself that leads and not any single individual.
- A spirit: The true spirit of community is the spirit of peace, love, wisdom and power. Members may view the source of this spirit as an outgrowth of the collective self or as the manifestation of a Higher Will.

The spiritual community of tomorrow will not be driven by the desire to raise money; therefore, there may not be a "meeting place" except in individual homes or common meeting places within the larger community. This de-emphasis on money will decrease the conflicts that fuel most church chaos and controversy. It will follow the practice of the early church members who met in homes to share common interests and concerns. They met whenever they had something to share. Many times people attending these meetings shared a common meal, much like the agape feasts of the early church, about which the Apostle Paul writes.

The spiritual community of the future will celebrate a concept called innate divinity that I talked about in chapter five. In the prologue of his book, *A Different Drum*, Peck tells a parable that he calls the "Rabbi's Gift." Peck paraphrases an unknown author in telling the story about a monastery that had fallen upon hard times. It was indeed a dying order until a visiting Rabbi suggested that the Messiah may be one of the members of the dying order. When each monk addressed their fellow monk with the thought, "Maybe Father Elred is the Messiah that the Rabbi was speaking of," then the change, of seeing the divinity in each other, began to occur. This new way of looking at each other changed the way they started treating each other. Eventually, the monastery began to flourish, new monks were added to the order, and the monastery became a vibrant center of light and spirituality in the realm.[214]

Spiritual seekers share this common theme that connects them with spiritual seekers of the ancient past. It will also act as a bridge between Christianity and other religions creating a more eclectic and ecumenical expression. This innate divinity found in the Rabbi's story is also characteristic of a concept called "perennial philosophy", a philosophy shared by not only the ancients from Egypt and Sumaria but also by many scientists and theologians worldwide. Aldous Huxley, in his book, *The Perennial Philosophy*, defines the phrase coined by Leibniz; "but the thing, the metaphysic that recognizes a divine Reality substantial to the world of things and lives and minds; the psychology that finds in the soul something similar to, or even identical with, divine Reality; the ethic that places man's final end in the knowledge of the immanent and transcendent Ground of all being—the thing is immemorial and universal. Rudiments of the Perennial Philosophy may be found among the traditionary lore of primitive peoples in every region of the world, and in its fully developed forms it has a place in every one of the higher religions"[215]

Traditionally, evangelical Christianity has been hostile towards the concept of perennial philosophy. To most evangelical Christians, their religion is the one true faith and it is exclusive. That is to say that anyone who is not of the Christian faith is denied salvation or those who are ignorant to Christianity will still be able to obtain salvation if they embrace the belief system of the Christian faith. However, perennial philosophy asserts that Christianity is only one of many religions, all of which are true faiths, and that non-Christians can achieve salvation without Christianity. The evidence in this book supports this claim. It is not surprising that this assertion has appeared to most evangelical Christians as heretical and contrary to their faith. In reality, perennial philosophy does not focus on salvation since the concept of innate divinity nullifies the need for any form of salvation.

Ken Wilber asserts that the perennial philosophy is not hostile to science, as so much of fundamentalism appears to be. Wilber suggests that many brilliant scientists have flirted with or totally embraced this philosophy, including Einstein, Schrodinger, Eddington, David Bohm and Isaac Newton. Wilber sums up the difference between this philosophy and salvation theology in the following quote: "The 'religion' of the perennial philosophy is quite different from salvation. Since the Ultimate is here pictured as an integral wholeness, the aim of this type of religion is not to be saved but to discover that wholeness. And thus, to find oneself whole as well."[216]

In America, religious spirituality of the future will give more attention to the content rather than the container. Ritual will take a back seat and experience or personal connection with God will dominate the religious landscape. When one's religion consists chiefly of a packaged philosophy to which one has given perfunctory assent, it is comparatively easy to handle without getting too involved. The comedian, Flip Wilson, quipped on one occasion; "I am a Jehovah bystander. They wanted me to become a Jehovah Witness, but I didn't want to get involved." It is impossible to be a bystander if you are a spiritual seeker. See side comment in notes.

# Chapter 22
# RECOVERING TRUE CHRISTIANITY

"Always take hold of things by the smooth handle."
Thomas Jefferson

Alvin Boyd Khun says in his book, *A Rebirth for Christianity*, "If Christianity will now recognize that the time has come to join with the other great religious traditions, and direct its vision to the reawakening of the divine spirit, the Christos in man, it may yet vindicate its right to call its message the true religion of humanity. Man must know that he is himself the universe in miniature, the microcosm, identical with the macrocosm that is the garment of God."[217]

The Greek word, "Christos" is the key to understanding the underlying principle that unites all people. Let's take a look at the Hebrew word that is translated "Christ" in the New Testament. It is the word that the Jews called "Messiah." In Isaiah, chapter 7, we find the reference to a child born to a young woman, whose name will be called Immanuel (God with us). This verse has been erroneously used by Christians to "prove" the virgin birth of Jesus. Listen to the text as it would colloquially be recited as Isaiah talks to Ahaz. "Ahaz, I have been calling my children by foreboding names, such as "Mahershalalhasbaz (take the money and run) and Shearjashub (only a remnant shall remain), but in the future that will change. Ahaz, do you see that pregnant woman in the field? Before she gives birth we will be calling our children, God with (within) us. This new child will have the freedom of choice "before the child shall know to refuse to choose evil and choose the good."[218] This choice is the key to change, the kind that will create the kind of transformation that we seek. The word "heretic" is correctly translated "the one who chooses." The heretic is the one who is totally free, the one who has extricated himself from the lies of those who seek to control. This is the one who has resisted the straitjacket of traditionalism, the one who sees himself as "the Christ"; this is the one on whom the future of Christianity rests.

Bishop John Shelby Spong has written a brilliant challenge for Christianity to change or die. He defines the alternative to the status quo as death. "Christianity was clearly, at its origins, designed and intended to be a radical, transforming, boundary breaking, religious experience. It was an invitation to enter into a new humanity without barriers, humanity without the defensive claims of tribal fear, a transformed humanity so full and free that God is perceived to be present within it. Jesus turned the values of his day upside down. He called people to follow in his path. To follow this man, we must put aside all our killing stereotypes based on external differences. He stood on the side of marginalized members of his society. He calls us to walk beyond our religious differences. He calls people to walk the path of wholeness into a new humanity. It was a path beyond every religious symbol and creed. Jesus calls us to journey into the full expression of our own humanity and into the mysteries of God. He possessed his life so fully, that he could give it away without undue fear. The cross, in this context, becomes the ultimate portrait of the redeeming power of love. Such a life becomes our doorway into the infinite. Jesus reveals the source of love, and then he calls us to enter it. He was not that source of life, but challenges us to live it as he lived it."[219]

The Catholic commentator, Daniel Gullotta, admires John Shelby Spong, although he does not support his theology. He asserts, "What draws me to Spong ultimately is our common enemy of literalism and fundamentalism. Spong has seen and experienced the appeal and danger of working in absolutes and certainties when it comes to faith and God. The dangerous fundamentalist ideology of: I have the truth, I know the truth, and only I have and know the truth—to whatever end, Spong exposes this ideology in literalist and fundamentalist thinking. There is a temptation and seduction in this way of thinking that has plagued the modern church, especially in a post-modern world that claims no absolutes—especially to young people seeking answers to the big questions. Spong challenges these certainties, not just theologically, but philosophically and physiologically. Spong warns that, 'All religion seems to need to prove that it's the only truth. And that's where it turns demonic. Because that's when you get religious wars and persecutions and burning heretics at the stake.'"[220]

Meister Eckhart (1260-1427), the German Dominican mystic who died before he could be fully tried for heresy by the archbishop of Cologne, once wrote that the Christ was not an historical person, per se, but rather "the collective soul of humanity." Carl Jung argued that only a "God within" had the much needed psychological power to transform human personality. Jung called this man, a human "imbued with a latent divinity." Our potential for Christhood and for experiencing the indwelling spirit of God is a reality that awaits our embrace. That the two, the divine concept and the human Jesus, were blended into one is a fact of history. Kuhn comments on this. "The question remains as to which direction the change tended. The first thesis is that Christianism took the human Jesus and made him to be very God; the second is that it took the Hellenic spiritual

Christos and personified into a human being, Jesus. A third solution is that the spiritual nonhuman Christos could have been humanized even if there had been no living figure of Jesus. The absence of any authentic, historical evidence of Jesus' existence argues strongly for this third suggestion."[221]

Marcus Borg is an example of a modern scholar who takes the Bible seriously. He, too, was brought up in fundamentalism and rejected it as a non-sensible relic of past accoutrements that strayed from the path of the original Galilean. The title of his book is *Meeting Jesus Again for the First Time*. Although he approaches the study of Jesus from the Jesus Seminar vantage point, he makes a passionate plea for Christians to explore what the latest biblical scholarship means for personal faith. "Believing in Jesus does not mean believing doctrines about him," Borg writes. "Rather, it means to give one's heart, one's self at its deepest level, to the living Lord." Drawing on his own journey from a naive, unquestioning belief in Jesus through collegiate skepticism to a mature and contemporary Christian faith, Borg illustrates how an understanding of a critical study of Jesus can actually lead to a more authentic Christian life, one not rooted in creeds or dogma, but in a life of spiritual challenge, compassion, and community. For questioning believers, doubters, and reluctant unbelievers alike, *Meeting Jesus Again for the First Time* frees our understanding of Jesus' life and message from popular misconceptions and outlines the way to a sound and contemporary faith. He concludes, "For ultimately, Jesus is not simply a figure of the past, but a figure of the present. Meeting that Jesus—the living one who comes to us even now—will be like meeting Jesus again for the first time."[222]

Although Jesus was not God-in-disguise, he stands head and shoulders above the teeming multitude who professes to worship him. He never saw himself as equal with God, and said so quite clearly, "I can do nothing of myself except the Father allows."[223] He viewed humanity as potential "gods" as recorded in John 10:34-38. I covered this verse in chapter five, when I discussed Jesus' teaching about innate divinity. He saw himself, primarily, as a teacher and a model for compassion, love and humility. His injunction was "follow me," not "worship me."

Harpur shares his personal reaction to his understanding of the pre-Christian symbols and the literal surface meaning by referring to their interpretation as a veneer which has glossed over the essential truths. He contends that the concepts at the heart of Christianity flow from the deep well of the unconscious, having been planted there by God. This idea of the "Christ within" to him and many others is an unmistakable Jungian style archetype in our human psyche. He says, "They are true because they ring with full authenticity on the anvil of our souls."[224]

A number of religious seekers seem to have difficulty distinguishing between pantheism (all is God), and panentheism, a term that defines the indwelling presence of God. Pantheism describes the presence of God in everything including rocks. In other words, God is the sum of all that is. Simply put, in pantheism, God is the whole, including all the parts, such as a raisin exists in the bread. In pantheism, God is identical to the Universe, or Nature. In contrast, panentheism shows us that all things exist in God. Each part contains the wholeness of God and is indistinguishable from God; and yet God is greater than the sum of the parts. My comments in chapter five about fractal science are an illustration of this distinction. This view moves us from a question of who or what God is to our experience of God as an active presence.

Panentheism is a term devised by Karl C. F. Krause (1781- 1832). Panentheism says that all is in God somewhat as if God were the ocean and we were a fish. Butterworth describes panentheism using the analogy of a drop of water in the ocean. We are the wave. God is the ocean. If we continue to say, as New Thoughters often do, that there is only one Presence and only one Power, God, the Good omnipotent, we should state it with an awareness of what it means in a panentheistic perspective. This affirmation may be made primarily as recognition that there is no Devil, no unified negative cosmic force in opposition to God; in other words, there is no opposing duality. When we say that there is only one Power and Presence, we are saying that the whole and the part are present in each other.

This understanding of God influenced the New England transcendentalists such as Ralph Waldo Emerson and Waldo Trine. Many Christians who believe in Universalism hold panentheistic views of God, following Emerson who was a major player in the New Thought Movement. New Thought includes Religious Science, Divine Science, and the Unity Church.[225] These groups hold as untenable the notion of a final and permanent alienation from God. They point to Biblical scripture passages such as Ephesians 4:6 "[God] is over all and through all and in all" and Romans 11:36 "from [God] and through him and to him are all things" to justify both panentheism and universalism.

Charles Hartshorne introduced his process theology in the 1940's, in which he examined, and discarded pantheism, deism, and pandeism in favor of panentheism, finding that such a doctrine contains all of deism and pandeism except their arbitrary negative aspects. The process school includes Alfred North Whitehead, who conceived of God as existing with all of reality (not prior to it), yet God is seen as the abiding source of all new possibilities. Paul Tillich referred to God as the "Ground of Being," a concept which identified God as the core of all that is. For Tillich, there was no imploring an external God to service our needs which is the core of Theism. These writers identify Theism as an outdated concept that requires new God images.

Thomas Merton is perhaps the greatest promoter of inter-spirituality. Merton, along with Father Matthew Fox, presents a theology that is steeped in panentheism. Fox calls for conversion to a new vision. "Embracing the cosmic Christ will require a paradigm shift...a shift from an anthropocentrism to a living cosmology, from Newton to Einstein, from parts mentality to wholeness, from rationalism to mysticism, from obedience as a prime moral virtue to creativity as a prime moral virtue, from personal salvation to communal healing; i.e. compassion as salvation from Theism (God outside us) to panentheism (God in us and us in God) from fall redemption religion to creation centered spirituality, from ascetic to aesthetic."[226]

The choice between Theism and Panentheism is one that will define the God debate of the future. Santiago Sia summarizes Hartshorne's panentheism:

"Panentheism...holds that God includes the world. But it sets itself apart from pantheism in that it does not maintain that God and the world are identical.... Hartshorne explains that God is a whole whose whole-properties are distinct from the properties of the constituents. While this is true of every whole, it is more so of God as the supreme whole.... The part is distinguishable from the whole although within it. The power of the parts is something suffered by the whole, not enacted by it. The whole has properties which are not shared by the parts. Similarly, God as whole possesses attributes which are not shared by his creatures.... We perpetually create content not only in ourselves but also in God. And this gives significance to our presence in this world."[227]

Can the skeptic be convinced to accept the major premise of this book, which is a renewed spirituality focused upon the ancient concept of the indwelling Christ? This is a question that I am convinced will be accepted in the affirmative by many who read this book. This understanding helps us move out of an outdated and irrelevant interpretation of Jesus' life and ministry into a universal connection between what he taught and what his ancient predecessor in antiquity taught. There are many questions that must be faced, such as the validity of the healing stories found in the Gospels. The New Testament miracles are virtually identical reproductions of ancient religious dramatizations, and not actual or historical occurrences.

Gerald Massey observes that the miracles of the gospels were the mythical of the Egyptian religion and subsequent Mysteries, all provably pre-extant. The healings are not to be dismissed as having no relevance. Viewed spiritually the message is powerful, since it communicates to us the reality that the Christ (or divinity) within each of us can be called upon to aid us in all our infirmities. When these stories are viewed in their true light, they will be seen as the power of God-healing energy that is not limited to the miraculous days of the New Testament, but is a present and available reality. The fourth Gospel writer calls Jesus' miracles signs that point to something else. That is the function of a sign. So the miracles of Jesus, as recorded in the Gospel of John, is a witness to the power of the indwelling Christ who is present to intoxicate humanity with the divine wine or the more abundant life that Jesus promised. This gives new meaning to the miracle of the changing of water into wine at the marriage of Cana which liberates the story from the charge of blatant forgery at the worst or a copy of the Bacchus or Horus prototype at the best. The Christ actually rivals and surpasses Bacchus (the Greek counterpart is Dionysus).

If the Book of John is read metaphysically, then the seven signs found in this book become a celebration of the new life that characterizes the spiritual, born-again person. Harpur comments about this transformation: "The fermented potency of wine was, at this deepest level, a symbol of the presence of the incarnated God within the spiritually aware person—direct contrast to the natural animal human. The transformation of water into wine represented the power of the divine to mature the inert elements of sense and feeling in every one of us into spiritual character. The Egyptians, and all those who closely followed them later, believed that each of us is intended ultimately to be a Christ, anointed for an eternal destiny with God."[228] This and other miracles found in the New Testament are metaphors for the spiritual process of allowing the innate presence of God to manifest.

The concept of being born twice is found in almost all early religions, including Hinduism. So, the new birth is not limited to a narrow interpretation of fundamentalism, but is so broad as to include a cosmic embrace of the infinite that transcends the personalized characterization of this principle in just one man, Jesus of Nazareth. The Egyptians, as well as many early Christians, believed that each of us is intended ultimately to be a Christ, anointed for an eternal destiny with God. The hope for true Christianity is found in this phrase, "Christ within you, your hope of glory."[229]

Since scripture is important to me, I close this chapter with verses that indicate this panentheistic teaching:

- "...even the highest heaven cannot contain God."[230]
- "Where could I go from your spirit? Or where could I flee from your presence? If I ascend to heaven, you are there. If I make my bed in Sheol, you are there. If I take the wings of the morning and settle at the farthest limits of the sea, even there your hand shall lead me and your right hand shall hold me fast."[231]
- "Do I not fill heaven and earth? Says the Lord."[232]
- "If these keep silence, the stones will cry out."[233]
- "All things came into being through the Word, And without the Word, not one thing came into being. What has come into being in the Word was life and the life was the light of all people."[234]
- Jesus said, "Split a piece of wood and I am there, lift up the stone ,and you will find me there."[235]
- "In this one we live and move and have our being."[236]
- "In Christ all things hold together."[237]

- "Christ is all in all."[238]
- " The fullness of the one who fills all in all."[239]
- "God is love, and those who abide in love abide in God and God in them."[240]

# Chapter 23
# CONCLUSION

"I have sworn upon the altar of God, eternal hostility
against every form of tyranny over the mind of man."
Thomas Jefferson (wall of his memorial, Washington, D.C.).

In 1970, while serving as professor of psychology at Ramey College in Puerto Rico, I had the privilege of meeting Viktor Frankl. My wife and I invited him to visit Ramey Air Force Base to speak to my classes. He graciously consented and spent two days lecturing to my students. I was impressed with him before this visit, but the time together cemented my positive impression of this intellectual and spiritual giant. In case you may not have heard of him, Frankl was a German psychiatrist, who survived the Nazi concentration camp. He lost his entire family in that holocaust. Part of the reason he survived was the mental and spiritual attitude that he developed while writing his book, *Man's Search for Meaning*. He wrote this book, while a prisoner, hiding the manuscript from his captors. He concluded that external circumstances may be beyond your control, but you can always choose your response to those events. What he learned in Auschwitz, was a key idea that he was already developing. Life is not a quest for pleasure, as Freud believes, or a quest for power, as Adler taught, but a quest for meaning. Frankl saw three possible sources for meaning: work, love and courage in difficult times. According to him, suffering in and of itself is meaningless; we give meaning to our suffering by the way that we respond to it. His life is a testimony to the claim that man's inner strength may raise him above his outer fate. You may not be able to control what happens to you, but you can always control how you feel and how you respond to what is happening.

A spirituality that does not provide a source of meaning for humanity does not deserve to survive. That is the reason why organized religion is becoming more and more impotent and irrelevant. It ignores the essential ingredient not only for survival, but also for a transformation of one's life in the process. That ingredient is meaning, as Frankl would define it, or purpose, as Rick Warren would define it. It is my conclusion that traditional religion in the West will become more and more irrelevant and lose whatever power it has sought to control, while religion in the East may be the demise of the Arab world, as fundamentalism defines Islam and controls the politics of the Arab states.

It is ironic that I close my book with a quote from the Apostle Paul, since I believe that it was he who subverted the original teachings of Jesus and replaced them with a substitute "Christianism." He eloquently penned these words: "Though I speak with the tongues of men and angels and have not love, I am a sounding brass and a tinkling symbol."[241] These words are easy to say and difficult to practice. The world of Jesus is a world where love is the fulcrum. When we are practicing the law of love, we choose to let each thought and action be an extension of God's love. To live in this consciousness requires a change in perception. Jampolsky reminds us that "when we choose to look at the world through the vision of love, in contrast to the ego's orientation, our belief in guilt and death comes to an end. We no longer confuse our identity with our bodies but instead, recognize the everlasting essence of our spiritual being."[242]

In the Greek New Testament there are three words for love. The word *eros* is an aesthetic or romantic love. However, in the Platonic dialogues *eros* is a yearning of the soul for the realm of the Divine. Love in this sense is not an emotion; it is a decision. The second word is *philia*, a reciprocal love and the intimate affection and friendship between friends. We love those whom we like and we love because we are love in return. The third word is *agape*, an understanding and redemptive good will for all men. This is an overflowing love which seeks nothing in return. *Agape* is the Love of God expressing in the human heart. Love cannot be identified by definition. The time must come when love is thought of in practical terms as a vital alternative to annihilation. The lessons of history have taught us something that we have not learned. Perish by our own hands or rise to a higher moral level through the grace of creative love. Both fear and love are choices that we must make. *A Course in Miracles* says: "What is not love is always fear, and nothing else."[243] Agape love is unconditional and unqualified.

If we do nothing more than talk about abstract principles without applying them in a practical way, we are participating in what Albert Ellis calls "mental masturbation." Our ideas about Love and God must meet the "rubber and road" litmus test. Unless we can relate to theological ideas in a meaningful way, we have managed to add to the layers of our B.S (Belief System). The question should always be, "do these ideas serve me and make my life meaningful and useful?" If our Belief System is so insecure and fragile that we find the need to defend it, then this is a good indication that we need to re-evaluate those ideas. Truth needs no defense, and we delude ourselves in thinking that God needs anything from us.

Without love, humans shrivel and die. Love opens the whole creation to life and calls all things into being. On the human level, love is the essential power that deepens our relationships and simultaneously expands our own humanity. The more we are freed by love to be ourselves, the more we are enabled to give our lives away to others. So, the call of this internal God found in our inner depths is a call to being what we were created to be. This understanding calls us to reject any religion that develops anything less than our full humanity. I am advocating a new agenda for the religious life that appears with this new understanding, this new way of seeing God. Institutional Christianity loses the power that it has derived from a traditional explanation of God with this new understanding.

Both Jesus and Paul talk about a child. Paul said, "When I was a child I spoke as a child."[244] Jesus said, "Except you become as a little child."[245] Paul's child is the child of the past that has been molded by our parents and significant other people in our lives. This child is simply a set of feelings and attitudes brought with us from childhood. This is the child that Paul would like to "put away." Jesus' child is the child of our essence. Jung called it the "Divine Child." This child refers to that part of each of us which is ultimately alive, energetic, creative, and fulfilled. It is our Real Self, who we truly are. This child is the "Christos" about which the great religions of the past spoke. Robert Frost wrote these words, "We sit around a ring and suppose, while the secret sits in the center and knows."[246] Jesus' inner child is the secret within that knows.

The Gnostics were probably the first Existential Christians who based their belief on an experience with the living Christ in contrast to Essentialist Christians who base their belief on faith in this Christ. Existentialism centers on the experience that necessitates an explanation. Essential Christianity focuses on the explanation and seeks to experience that explanation through practice or duplication, which often results in hypocrisy or frustration. It is my conclusion that "Christianism" is a non sequitur, but there is little humor in the conclusions that have been universally accepted as truth.

Since much of "Christianism" is based on illogical statements and beliefs, it is my position that Jesusonian Christianity or primitive Christianity offers a better way of blending the mind with the heart which is exactly what we find in the teachings of Jesus. Teilhard de Chardin closes his book with these sublime words: "Someday after we have mastered the winds, the waves, the tides and gravity, we will harness for God the energies of love, and then for the second time in the history of the world, man will have discovered fire."[247]

Where does all this leave me, regarding my theological orientation? To say that I am a heretic is a correct appellation, since the original meaning of the word is choice. I have made a choice to move beyond my fundamentalist background and training to pursue an open evaluation of the available evidence in a spirit of unimpeded freedom. Where does this leave the traditional Christian who is willing to embrace the evidence that I have presented in this book? Does it leave him/her as a ship without a sail or a boat without a rudder? At times it does feel that way since the realization of uncertainty and insecurity is a helpless feeling. The human tendency is for someone to rescue us, to be our Savior. The pursuit of truth leaves one adrift, but free. It is this freedom that prompted Jefferson to say in a letter to James Smith in 1822, "Man once surrendering his reason, has no remaining guard against absurdities the most monstrous, and like a ship without rudder, is the sport of every wind."[248] So the real rudderless life is the one that swallows the teachings of traditional Christianity without critical examination and defends them with the passion of an emotion that has been born out of capitulation to these dogmas. In other words, they have swallowed the "blue pill." My plea is to "take the red pill." When you do, you will take the "Road Not Taken" as expressed by the poet Robert Frost. Scott Peck called it a "road less traveled" in a book he wrote by that title. I hope that my book will swell the ranks of those who walk this road.

Two roads diverged in a yellow wood,
And sorry I could not travel both
And be one traveler, long I stood
And looked down one as far as I could
To where it bent in the undergrowth;
Then took the other, as just as fair,
And having perhaps the better claim,
Because it was grassy and wanted wear;
Though as for that the passing there
Had worn them really about the same,
And both that morning equally lay
In leaves no step had trodden black.
Oh, I kept the first for another day!
Yet knowing how way leads on to way,
I doubted if I should ever come back.
I shall be telling this with a sigh
Somewhere ages and ages hence:
Two roads diverged in a wood, and I-
I took the one less traveled by,
And that has made all the difference.

From the album by Jackson Browne, there is a song entitled "For a Dancer" that talks about the dance that most people do, one that is choreographed by others. These are the steps that are dictated by culture, religion, society, family, etc. Most of us are doing the steps that we've been shown by everyone we've ever known, and often we don't realize that we are still dancing to those tunes as adults. The lyrics of this song suggest that we must learn to toss some seed of our own, and become the choreographer of our own lives, dancing to the tune that we compose.

I close with a brief quote from the lyrics by Jackson Browne in his song, "For a Dancer."

Into a dancer you have grown from a seed somebody else has thrown

Go on ahead and throw some seeds of your own
And somewhere between the time you arrive and the time you go
May lie a reason you were alive but may never know.

———————

# Bibliography

Acharya, S (a.k.a. D.M. Murdock) *The Christ Conspiracy: The Greatest Story Ever Sold*, Kempton, IL: Adventures Unlimited, 1999.

Akers, Keith, *The Lost Religion of Jesus*, New York: Lantern Books, 2000.

Anonymous, *A Course in Miracles*, New York: Foundation for Inner Peace, 1977.

Bach, Richard, *Jonathan Livingston Seagull*, New York: Scribner, 1970.

Beckett, Samuel, *Waiting for Godot*, New York: Grove Press, 1954.

Bonhoeffer, Dietrich, *The Cost of Discipleship*, New York: Touchstone Press, 1959.

Borg, Marcus, *Reading the Bible Again for the First Time*, San Francisco: Harper Collins Paperback Edition, 2002.

Borg, Marcus, *Meeting Jesus Again for the First Time*, New York: Harper Collins paperback, 1994.

Borg, Marcus and John Dominic Crossan, *The First Paul*, New York: Harper Collins, 2009.

Braden, Greg, *The Divine Matrix*, New York: Hay House, 2010.

Brown, Dan, *The Da Vinci Code*, New York: Doubleday, 2003.

Brown, Raymond E., *An Introduction to the New Testament*, New York: Doubleday, 1996.

Buber, Martin, *I and Thou*, New York: Charles Scribner Son, 1970.

Butterworth, Eric, *Discover the Power within You*, New York: Harper Collins Paperback Edition, 1992.

Campbell, Joseph, *The Power of Myth*, New York: Doubleday, 1988.

Cady, Emile, *How I Used Truth*, Lee's Summit, Missouri: Unity Press.

Chardin, Teilhard de, *The Phenomenon of Man*, New York: Harper, 1964.

Ehrman, Bart, *Misquoting Jesus*, San Francisco: Harper, 2005.

Ehrman, Bart, *Jesus Interrupted*, New York: Harper One, 2009.

Ehrman, Bart, *Forged: Writing in the Name of God—Why the Bible's Authors Are Not Who We Think They Are*, New York: Harper One, 2011.

Ehrman, Bart, *Did Jesus Exist?*, New York: Harper One, 2012.

Eisenbaum, Pamela, *Paul Was Not A Christian*, New York: Harper One, 2009.

Emerson, Ralph Waldo, *The Complete Writings of Ralph Waldo Emerson*, New York: William Wise and Co.

Errico, Rocco, *Setting A Trap for God*, Unity Village, Missouri: Unity House, 1997.

Fillmore, Charles, *Talks On Truth*, Lee's Summit, Missouri: Unity Press.

Findlay, Authur, *The Psychic Stream*, London: Psychic Press, 1947.

Fox, Matthew, *The Coming of the Cosmic Christ*, New York: Harper and Row, 1988.

Frankl, Viktor, *Man's Search for Meaning*, New York: Beacon Press, 1992.

Freke, Timothy and Gandy, Peter, *The Laughing Jesus*, New York: Harmony House Books, 2005.

Funk, Robert W., Roy W. Hoover, and the Jesus Seminar, *The Five Gospels*: What Did Jesus Really Say? San Francisco: Harper, 1993.

Godsey, R. Kirby, *Is God A Christian?* Macon: Mercer University Press, 2011.

Godsey, R. Kirby, *When We Talk About God Let's Be Honest,* Macon: Smyth & Helwys Pub., Inc. 1996.

Grof, Stanislav, *Beyond the Brain,* Albany: State University of New York, 1985.

Hall, Manly P., *The Lost Keys of Freemasonry,* Jeremy Tracher/Penguin, 1950.

Harpur, Thomas, *The Pagan Christ,* New York: Thomas Allen Publishers, 2004.

Hicks, Esther and Jerry, *The Law of Attraction,* Carlsbad, CA.: 2006.

Hoeller, Stephan, *The Gnostic Jung,* New York: Quest Books, 1982.

Hoff, Benjamin, *The Tao of Pooh,* New York: Penguin Books, 1982.

Huxley, Aldous, *The Perennial Philosophy,* New York: Harper, 1970.

Jackson, John G., *Christianity Before Christ,* American Atheist Press, Austin, Texas, 1985.

Jampolsky, Gerald, *Teach Only Love,* Hillsboro, Oregon: Beyond Words Publishing, 1983.

Jenkins and LaHaye, *Left Behind,* Wheaton: Tyndale House Publishers, 1995.

Johnson, James Weldon, *God's Trombones,* New York: Penguin Books, 1927.

Keck, L. Robert, *Sacred Eyes,* Indianapolis: Knowledge Systems, Inc., 1992

Kuhn, Alvin Boyd, *Shadow of the Third Century*, Filiquarian Publishing, LLC, 2007.

Kuhn, Alvin Boyd, *Who is this King of Glory?* Zuu Books.

Kuhn, Alvin Boyd, *A Rebirth for Christianity*, Quest Books, 1970.

Lewis, C.S. *Mere Christianity*, New York: MacMillan Company, 1952.

Marrs, Jim, *Rule by Secrecy*, New York: Harper Collins Publishers, 2000.

Martyr, Justin, *The Apologies of Justin Martyr,*

Nicoll, Maurice, *The Mark*, Shambala, Boston & London, 1985.

Pagels, Elaine, *Beyond Belief*, New York: Vintage Books, 2004.

Pagels, Elaine, *The Gnostic Gospels*, New York: Random House, 1979.

Paine, Thomas, *The Age of Reason*, New York: Citadel Press, 1948.

Pearce, Joseph Chilton, *The Death of Religion and the Re-Birth of Spirit*, Rochester: Park Street Press, 2007.

Pearce, Joseph Chilton, *The Biology of Transcendence*, Rochester: Park Street Press, 2002.

Peck, M. Scott, *The Different Drum*, New York: Simon and Schuster, 1987.

Peck, M. Scott, *People of the Lie*, New York: Simon and Schuster, 1983.

Peck, M.Scott, *The Road Less Traveled*, New York: Simon and Schuster, 1988.

Ryce, Michael, *Why Is this Happening to me again*, Self-published, Theodosia, Missouri, 1997.

Sanford, John, *The Kingdom Within*, New York: Harper Collins, 1987.

Schweitzer, Albert, *Quest For the Historical Jesus*, Minneapolis: Fortress Press, 2001.

Sheldon, Charles, *In His Steps*, Revised by Harold Chadwick, New Jersey: Bridge-Logos, 1999.

Shepherd, Thomas, *Friends in High Places*, Lincoln, NE: iUniverse, Inc. 2004.

Smith, Paul R., *Integral Christianity*, St. Paul, MI:Paragon House, 2011.

Spong, John Shelby, *Why Christianity Must Change or Die*, New York: Harper Collins Paperback Edition, 1998.

Spong, John Shelby, *Rescuing the Bible from Fundamentalism*, New York: Harper Collins Paperback Edition.

Spong, John Shelby, *Jesus for the Non-Religious*, New York: Harper Collins Paperback Edition, 2007.

Spong, John Shelby, *The Sins of Scripture*, San Francisco: Harper Collins Paperback Edition, 2005.

Spong, John Shelby, *A New Christianity for a New World*, San Francisco: Harper Collins Paperback Edition, 2001.

Talbot, Michael. *The Holographic Universe*. New York: Harper Collins, 1991.

Turner, Elizabeth Sand, *Your Hope of Glory*, Lee's Summit, Missouri, Unity Press.

Wilber, Ken, *Up From Eden*, Boston: New Science Library, 1986.

Wilber, Ken, *Integral Spirituality: A Startling New Role for Religion in the Modern and Postmodern world*. Boston: Shambhala, 2006.

Williams, Margery, *The Velveteen Rabbit*, New York: Doubleday, 1922.

# Endnotes

1    Fundamentalists have an uneasy feeling about the success of their Orthodox Christianity with the most obvious expression of that angst seen in their defensiveness. A recent letter to the editor in my local paper illustrates this internal conflict. The writer was rebutting a plea made by one writer for more tolerance in the Christian community. I quote from his article, "All the knowledge mankind has obtained over thousands of years has not made us better people. In fact I would tend to believe that it has made mankind more self-centered and wicked." If the Christian faith is not designed to make us a "better people," then what is it for?

2    Buber, *I and Thou*

3    Wilber, *Integral Philosophy*

4    I Corinthians 13:11

5    Pearce, *The Biology of Transcendence*

6    Pearce, *the Death of Religion and the Re-Birth of Spirit*
The subtitle of this book is revealing. It is "A return to the intelligence of the heart." Pearce was a faculty member on child development at the Jung Institute in Switzerland. More recently, he has become a certified Heart-Math trainer, further developing his already extensive insights into the heart-brain connection. This connection between the heart and brain is not merely neurological and autonomic, or romantic and meta-

phoric—it is central to our full development and total health.

7    Luke 15:17
8    Socrates left no writings of his own, thus our awareness of his teachings comes primarily from a few ancient authors who referred to him in their own works.
9    Romans 12:22
10   II Peter 2:18
11   The book of Job in the Old Testament
12   Acts 26:28
13   Genesis 34:25
14   Exodus chapters 5-12
15   II Kings 6:1-7
16   Joshua 6
17   Joshua 10:12-14
18   Exodus 14:21-22
19   Numbers 22:28
20   Deuteronomy 28
21   Genesis 19:15
22   Exodus 7:12
23   Judges 6:39
24   Judges 16:26-30
25   14 Deut. 7:2, 7:16 and 20:12-17; Ps. 1:4-9; Isa. 9:17-20; Jer 20:1615 Gen. 9:20-25, 20:18; Ex. 12:29-30, 20:5; Lev. 21:17-21; Deut. 5:9; 1st Sam. 3:11-14; 2nd Sam. 5:8; Job 1:1-19, 2:1-7, 30:20-31; and Isa. 14:2
26   Deuteronomy 7:2 And when the LORD thy God shall deliver them before thee; thou shalt smite them, and utterly destroy them; thou shalt make no covenant with them, nor shew mercy unto them.
27   Deuteronomy 7:3
28   Song of Solomon
29   Rylands Library Papyrus, pg. 52
30   Erhman, *The New Testament: An Historical Introduction to The Early Christian Writings*, p. 449

31  Josephus Book XII, Chapter 11

32  I Corinthians 13: 9-12
33  Kuhn, *Shadow of the Third Century* pg. 8
34  Harpur *The Pagan Christ*, pg, 147.
35  Campbell, *The Power of Myth*, pg. 199.
36  Luke 6:41-42
37  John 5:30
38  Mark 9:1-9
39  Mark 16:8
40  29 Brown, A Risen Christ in Eastertime: Essays on the Gospel Narratives of the Resurrection (all of Browns books can be found on Amazon.com with used copies under $4.00 each.)
41  http://www.traditionalmass.org/images/articles/Raz-ResArt.pdf
42  I Corinthians 15
43  32 Luke 24:13-35
44  Gen 18
45  Gen 19
46  I Corinthians 15:5
47  Codex Bezea is a codex of the New Testament dating from the 5th century written in an uncial hand on vellum.
48  John 20:19
49  John 21:1-25
50  Matthew 5:14
51  Smith, *Integral Christianity*, pgs. 331-334
52  Williams, Margery, *The Velveteen Rabbit*
53  Shepherd, *Friends in High Places*, pg. xxi
54  For a detailed examination of these theories, read Bart Ehrman's *Misquoting Jesus*, pages 155-174)
55  Ehrman, *Did Jesus Exist?* Pgs. 14-34
56  Murdock, *The Christ Conspiracy: The Greatest Story Ever Sold.*
57  Romans 8:15

58  Galatians 4:5
59  Mark 8:27-30
60  Matthew. 13:55 and 27:56
61  Luke 17:21
62  Matthew 17:20
63  Johnson, *God's Trombones*, pg. 21
64  Luke 9:62
65  Luke 15:11-32
66  Turner, *Your Hope of Glory*, pg.17
67  *Masterpieces of Religious Verse* pg. 431
68  The Peale in this pithy phrase is Norman Vincent Peale, the guru of the Positive thinking movement.
69  Galatians 4:4
70  Col 1:27-28
71  Galatians 2:20
72  I Corth 6:19, Gal. 4:19, I Corth. 3:16, Eph 3:17, I John 4:4
73  Pseudipigrapha is an antiseptic term used by scholars to depict a literary lie.
74  Ehrman, *Forged: Writing in the Name of God*
75  Borg and Crossan, *The First Paul*, pgs. 13-16
76  Philemon 16-20
77  I Timothy 2:11-15
78  Wings of Song, pg. 65
79  John 10:33
80  Psalm 82:6
81  Smith, Integral Christianity, pg. 203
82  John 10:34
83  John 14:12
84  *Ibid*
85  *Ibid*, pg. 206
86  Genesis 1:26
87  Isaiah 7:16
88  Luke 17:21
89  John 9:5
90  Matthew 5:14
91  Matthew 7:13

92    John 17:20
93    Fox, *The Cosmic Christ*, pg. 25
94    I John 3:2
95    II Corinthians 3:18
96    Hebrews 2:17
97    Quote about fractal science is taken from Wikipedia
98    *Ibid*, pg. 216
99    Mark 10:18
100   Fillmore, *Talks on Truth* pg.169
101   Cady, *How I Used Truth*, pg. 21
102   Kuhn, *A Rebirth for Christianity*, pg. 70
103   Hicks, *The Law of Attraction*, pg. 20
104   Spong, *Why Christianity Must Change or Die*, pg.86
105   Harpur, *The Pagan Christ* Notes pg. 227
106   Hebrews 11:1
107   Mark 9:24
108   Matt. 8:10; Luke 5:20 Mark 11:22
109   Romans 3
110   Matthew 10:34-39
111   The Urantia Book
112   Micah 6:8
113   Galatians 5:12
114   Pagels, *The Gnostic Gospels* pgs. 7-8
115   *Ibid*, pg. 151
116   Mark 4:10-12
117   Pagels, *The Gnostic Gospels*, pg.150
118   Hall, *Doctrine of Antiquity* pg. 76
119   Akers, *The Lost Religion of Christianity*
120   Marrs, *Rule by Secrecy*, pg. 351
121   Found in Gelasius, Church History 3.19.1 Trans: Coleman-Norton, P.R., Roman State and Christian Church, London: Society for Promoting Christian Knowledge (SPCK) 1966, #67.
122   Wace, A Dictionary of Christian Biography and Literature to the End of the Sixth Century, A.D., with an Account of the Principal Sects and Heresies

123  The Irim and Thummin is a bizarre method that the priests used in the Hebrew era to determine the "vote" of God on a certain subject.. When they wanted to know the will of God, they would toss the Urim and Thummin, or sacred dice. Clear examples of this procedure are found in I Samuel 23:9-12; 30:7-8. In the first instance David asked the priest Abiathar to bring the ephod or Urim and Thummim. David used these sacred dice to address two direct questions to God. The exact meaning of the words is not known. According to the texts the Urim and Thummim were deposited in the "breastpiece", a small, square pocket made of multicolored material which the chief priest carried on his "heart" above the ephod. The "breast piece was attached to the ephod, and hence the latter term was in some cases used as a synonym for the Urim and Thummim. This information would suggest that the Urim and Thummiom were small objects, perhaps in the shape of dice, having some symbols impressed on them. The symbols were necessarily reduced to a single letter or sign on each object; e.g., "a" representing an affirmative response and "b" a negative one—and accordingly interpreted by the priest in charge. In complicated issues the divinatory media were used several times in order to decide the case. The technique employed by the priest in handling the Urim and Thummim is not stated. Since they were kept in a pocket, the priest either shook them in the receptacle and then pulled one out or used the same method as in the case of the "lots"—namely, he "cast" both of them on the ground or on any other surface. The use of "lots" in the selection of the replacement of Judas as the twelfth disciple is reminiscent of the use of the Urim and Thummim. It is obvious, as we will argue that the Christian Church had its roots in Judaism and therefore it is not surprising that they would employ an ancient device in deter-

mining the will of God when they selected Matathias, as the twelfth disciple.

124   Harpur, *The Pagan Christ* pg. 10

125   Kuhn, *Who is this King of Glory?*, Introduction
126   Hoeller, *The Gnostic Jung*, pg.11
127   Augustine, Retractions. I, xiii quoted by Kuhn, *Shadow of the Third Century*, pg. 18
128   Augustine, Retractions. I, xiii quoted by Kuhn, *Shadow of the Third Century*, pg. 18
129   *Ibid*, pg. 19
130   Justin Martyr, *The Apologies of Justin Martyr* chapter 59
131   Harpur, *The Pagan Christ*, pg. 63
132   Colossians 1:27
133   Kuhn, *Who Is This King of Glory* pg. 6
134   Pagels, *The Gnostic Gospels*, pg. xx
135   The first step in the work of the Jesus Seminar was to inventory and classify all the words attributed to Jesus found in the Gospels. The Seminar collected more than fifteen hundred versions of approximately five hundred items for examination. The items were classified under four categories: parables, aphorisms, dialogues, and stories containing words attributed to Jesus. The inventory included all the surviving Gospels from every source in the first three centuries of the Common Era (C.E.). The Seminar refused to be bound by the limitations of the canonical gospels, in other-words the Synoptic Gospels and John.
The goal of the Seminar was to examine the material in the surviving gospels and determine with a high degree of probability what words could be ascribed to Jesus. The scholars had to decide how to reach its decisions and then how they would report the results to the general public. Voting was the method agreed upon by the group as the most efficient way of reaching a

consensus. This method may appear to be arbitrary to most Bible novices, but it has a long history of usage in the establishment of the New Testament canon. The New Testament was "officially" compiled by the vote of church leaders in session, with the Council of Nicaea in 325 C.E. being the cutoff point. Every translation of the New Testament by a committee has been subjected to this method of consensus voting. They simply voted on what to include in the text and what to reject. Voting does not guarantee accuracy; it only indicates the best judgment of the scholars assigned to a particular text. The Seminar scholars dropped colored beads into a voting box in order to maintain secrecy. The seminar adopted a model of four categories to identify the words of Jesus. A red bead suggested that Jesus did in fact say it. This material would help in determining who Jesus was and what he taught. A pink bead represented reservations about the degree of certainty or some question about changes that were incurred in the course of its transmission and recording. Pink identifies words that sound like Jesus. A gray bead was probably not authentic, but would be helpful in determining who Jesus was. In other words, Jesus did not say this, but the ideas are close to his own. The black beads definitely indicated that Jesus did not say this. This material represented the theological development of the early church, such as the material found in the Gospel of John. The ballots were ranked by weighted vote, which would allow all votes to count under this method of counting. In a system of winners and losers, nearly half of the Fellows would lose their vote. Under the system used by the Seminar, all votes would count in the averages.

The inspiration for this new "red letter edition" came from a German publisher who conceived the idea for printing the words of Jesus in red, the color of his blood.

Funk tells us about a fourteenth century manuscript of the four gospels written in Greek and Latin that anticipated the red 0letter editions of later times. This narrative text of the manuscript was written by hand in vermilion, while the words of Jesus are written in crimson. This document is known as Codex 16 and is located in the Bibliotheque Nationale in Paris.

136    Tom Harpur, *The Pagan Christ,* pp.133-135
137    Ibid, pg. 135
138    Augustine, De nupt. et concup., II, xxvi, 43.
139    *Catholic Encyclopedia* Online article.
140    Bozarth, in the *American Atheist,* Sept 1979, pg. 30.
141    Psalm 8:3-4
142    Genesis 1:27
143    Bach, *Jonathan Livingston Seagull,* pg. 13.
144    Galatians 4:4
145    II Samuel 13 1ff
146    Joshua 2:1
147    Ruth 1:1
148    1 Kings 1:11
149    John 10:10
150    http://www.brainyquote.com/quotes/authors/p/pablo_casals.html
151    Wilde, *Miracles,* pg. 1
152    John 14:12
153    Poem by William Blake, quoted by Gregg Braden in *The Divine Matrix: Bridging Time, Space, Miracles, and Belief.*
154    John 3:8
155    Hebrews 3:1
156    John 10:8
157    Thomas Jefferson, letter to Dr. Thomas Cooper, from Monticello, February 10, 1814
158    Deut. 7:1-2
159    1 Samuel 15
160    1 Samuel 17

161  Numbers 25::7-8
162  Numbers 25:10-13
163  Numbers 25:8-9
164  1 Kings 18
165  Numbers 15:32-36
166  Ephesians 4:28
167  Matthew 19:16-19
168  Matt. 22:324-40
169  Matthew 19:16-19
170  Hoff, *The Tao of Pooh*, back of cover
171  Holmes, "Light of Asia Review" The International Review #7
172  Godsey, *Is God a Christian?* Macon: Mercer Press, Pg. 38
173  *Ibid*, Pg. 41
174  Power is your ability to choose your thoughts and consequently directly affect your feelings. You have the power of choice over anger and fear to supplant them with compassion and courage. Unfortunately, you have been programmed with sets of ideas and emotions that have been repeated so many times that they are deeply ingrained. One of these beliefs is that it is difficult to change patterns of thoughts and feelings. This is not true, according to Hawkins. The truth is that most people basically do not want to change. But the ability to change, nevertheless, is there. When you realize that you have this tremendous power, you can change your thoughts and emotions at will. Why don't we do it more often if the benefits are obviously helpful and healthy? The answer is homeostasis, the balancing system that is built into your body. Most of the time homeostasis is very beneficial and is the reason we are able to heal. However, if you want to change, you have to overcome homeostasis, which is the force that keeps your condition at familiar levels. Our goal should be to recognize and use our wonderful gift of power as

a spiritual tool in consciousness development to draw upon it in order to bring more spiritual awareness into the consciousness of mankind.

175  Acts 17:28
176  Works of Gurdjieff
177  The work of "self-observation" is central to Gurdjieff's teaching and acquires a completely new meaning as the developing attention lets go of its effort, joining and willingly submitting to a higher conscious seeing. The action that might take place in this condition—in the quiet of meditation or even in outer action—reflects the simultaneous dual nature of both an impersonal consciousness and a personal attention which has a new capacity to manifest and act in the world. The qualities of both these aspects of consciousness and attention are quite unknown to the ordinary mind. In this new relationship of individual attention and a higher impersonal consciousness, a man or woman can become a vessel, serving another energy which can act through the individual, an energy which at the same time transforms the materiality of the body at the cellular level.

It is not easy to observe one's self. This is the reason why the work is difficult. It requires effort and effort is not something that the average person enjoys or is willing to participate. If in his writings Gurdjieff never sought merely to lay out a philosophical system, all the more in his direct work with pupils did he mercilessly resist the role of guru, preacher, or school teacher? Man, Gurdjieff taught, is an unfinished creation. He is not fully Man, considered as a cosmically unique being whose intelligence and power of action mirror the energies of the source of life itself. On the contrary, man, as he is, is an automaton. Our thoughts, feelings, and deeds are little more than mechanical reactions to external and internal stimuli. In Gurdjieff's terms, we cannot do anything.

In and around us, everything "happens" without the participation of an authentic consciousness. But human beings are ignorant of this state of affairs because of the pervasive and deeply internalized influence of culture and education, which engrave in us the illusion of autonomous conscious selves. In short, man is asleep. There is no authentic I am in his presence, but only a fractured egoism which masquerades as the authentic self, and whose machinations poorly imitate the normal human functions of thought, feeling, and will. Many factors reinforce this sleep. Each of the reactions that proceed in one's presence is accompanied by a deceptive sense of I—one of many I's, each imagining itself to be the whole, and each buffered off from awareness of the others. Each of these many I's represents a process whereby the subtle energy of consciousness is absorbed and degraded, a process that Gurdjieff termed "identification." Man identifies—that is, squanders his conscious energy, with every passing thought, impulse, and sensation. This state of affairs takes the form of a continuous self-deception and a continuous procession of egoistic emotions, such as anger, self-pity, sentimentality, and fear, which are of such a pervasively painful nature that we are constantly driven to ameliorate this condition through the endless pursuit of social recognition, sensory pleasure, or the vague and unrealizable goal of "happiness."

178   Matthew 13:11, Mark 4:11 and Luke 8:10
179   II Corinthians. 5:17
180   Bonheoffer, *The Cost of Discipleship*, pg. 53
181   *Ibid* pg. 54
182   Matthew 7:12 and Luke 6:31
183   Luke 9:62
184   Kunh, *A Rebirth for Christianity*, Pg. 234
185   C.G Jung, *The collected works* vol. 12, pgs. 7-8 (Kuhn quotes idea)

186  Spong, *Why Christianity Must Change or Di,e.* pg, 26
187  *Ibid*, pg. 120
188  John 14:12
189  John 10:34
190  Errico, *Setting a Trap for God: The Aramaic Prayer of Jesus*, pg. 7.
191  Psalm 42:1
192  Butterworth, *Discover the Power Within*, Pg. 106
193  Matthew 6:1-6
194  Emerson, *The Complete Writings Ralph Waldo of Emerson* pg. 148
195  Personal e-mail from Dr. Ryce
196  Daniel 11:36-45
197  Daniel 11:39a
198  Revelation 14:19-21:
199  Revelation 13:16-18
200  Revelation: 19:20
201  Luke 23:43
202  Revelation 20
203  Daniel 9:27
204  Beckett, Waiting for Godot
205  Findlay, *The Psychic Stream*, pp. 209-211
206  Mark 8:27-33
207  http://www/stanleykrippner.com  /papers/basel-the future of religion-revised.htm
208  Chardin, The Phenomena of Man
209  Quoted in Ken Wilber's *Up From Eden*, pg. 6
210  Grof, *Beyond the Brain*, pg. 26
211  John 20:22
212  Ryce, *Why Is This Happening to me Again?*
213  Peck, *The Different Drum*, chapter one
214  *The Different Drum* was written by Scott Peck. He did not write this story. He paraphrased it.
215  Huxley, *The Perennial Philosophy*
216  Wilber, *Up From Eden*, pgs. 3-7
217  Khun, *A Rebirth for Christianity*, pg. 248

218   Isaiah 7:16
219   Spong, Why Christianity must change or Die
220   Gullotta, Internet article www. Catholica.org
221   Kuhn, A Rebirth for Christianity, Pg. 187
222   Marcus Borg, Meeting Jesus Again for the first Time, pg. 3
223   John 5:30
224   Harpur, The Pagan Christ, Pg. 47
225   Since I have identified myself as a Unity Minister, the reader may be wondering what my assessment is of that movement and where it fits within my present philosophy? I am grateful for my stage-appropriate experience with the Unity Church of Christianity, but I find some weaknesses in that over-all approach to Jesusonian Christianity that I am championing. First, with its emphasis on "prosperity thinking" one would think that most Unity folks would be wealthy. The opposite is true. Unity churches are struggling to pay their ministers and many are folding because they cannot survive economically. This emphasis on prosperity tends to be spirituality in service of the ego. Another teaching of Unity, that I question, is the teaching that our thoughts create reality. This is partial truth. When taken as gospel, this teaching can be dangerous. A correlate to this teaching is "consciousness creates reality." One writer asks, "Whose consciousness?" Other people impact our lives in significant ways and affect the consequences dramatically. Part of our reality is created by circumstances beyond our control. In 2008, I lost my entire portfolio and my business, including my residence and my retirement. I do not claim responsibility for every aspect of that loss. I do own what was my part of that loss, thus accept some responsibility. The major part of that loss was the economic condition that existed in Florida at that time. It is possible that "life is consciousness" is an absolute teaching with my failure representing my level of consciousness at that time.

Part of reality is created by the natural order of the material world. Tornadoes and floods are not created by our thinking or consciousness, but by the natural order. The real teaching of Unity is how we think and deal with these circumstances that are beyond our control. Maintaining a positive attitude through troubling times is a hallmark of Unity's teachings. I am concerned by the tendency in some Unity churches to be embarrassed by any reference to Jesus. This movement was founded on the teachings of Jesus and this tendency is disturbing. The church of the future, that I embrace, is rooted and grounded in the life, teachings and presence of Jesus. In general Unity people are free to shop around for any belief and practice that either fits them or feels good. This freedom excludes the aspect of commitment to the community, which is fundamental to an evolving expression of Integral Christianity. As a result, conflict within the church results in a scattering of the flock. Unity Churches have not learned to deal creatively with conflict. When I was minister in Sarasota, conflict seemed to be the order of the day. We had Tom Crum, author of the *Magic of Conflict,* as a guest to assist us in this growth process. His teaching was illuminating and may have made some impact, but ego-centered behavior on both the part of the minister and some members trumped the ultimate outcome. The embrace of New Age ideas without discernment seems to be another flaw of the Unity Movement. what New Agers call channeling is a valid Biblical concept; however it is easy to accept any spirit communication without a proper compass and rudder. The compass and rudder of my position is the teaching of Jesus which is characterized by love and compassion. There has been a tendency in recent years for Unity to evaluate its members and clergy by the degree to which they were true to the "fundamentals of Unity." This understanding is a violation of the consciousness and teachings of its founders, Charles and Myrtle Fillmore. Yet, judgment as to whether one is a "real Unity Minister" is prevalent in a number of Unity Churches. In my opinion, there is only one litmus test for true Unity. That is a belief in and the practice of innate divinity.

226  Fox, *The Coming of the Cosmic Christ*, pg. 57
227  Sia, God in Process Thought, pg. 21
228  Harpur, *The Pagan Christ*, Pg. 100-101
229  Colossians 1:27

230  II Chronicles 2:6
231  Jeremiah 23:24
232  Luke 19:40
233  John 12-4
234  Gospel of Thomas Saying 77
235  Acts 17:28
236  Colossians 1:17
237  Colossians 3:16
238  Ephesians 1:23
239  Ephesians 4:6
240  I John 4:16
241  I Corinthians 13:1
242  Jampolsky, *Teach only Love*
243  A Course in Miracles
244  I Corinthians 13
245  Matthew 18:3
246  http://www.brainyquote.com/quotes/quotes/r/robert-fros151827.
247  Chardin, *The Phenomena of Man*, pg. 297
248  Jefferson quote

Made in the USA
Charleston, SC
01 November 2012